No Right Field
For My Son:

A Dad Pushes Too Hard

JOE RECTOR

Copyright © 2012 Joe Rector
All rights reserved.

ISBN: 0983219818
ISBN 13: 9780983219811

Joe Hester

I am grateful and thankful for my wife Amy and daughter Lacey for putting up with me over the years. I also thank Judy Tharpe, who edited this book. Most of all, I thank my son Dallas for surviving the ordeals related in this book and for loving me in spite of my actions. I hope he knows they were done with the best of intentions.

PREFACE

So this is the way the whole thing ends—with a whimper instead of a bang. An entire lifetime has come down to this one evening. In so many ways this day symbolizes the entire time.

It started out with overcast skies, and the weatherman predicted afternoon and evening thundershowers. Grayness all day and the worry that the final game would be a rainout sucked the life out of what should have been a joyous occasion.

Monday evening was to be senior night for the boys. After four years of playing ball, their night had come, the one where the crowd could recognize their efforts and give them an ovation. After all, this group had tied for the regular season district championship and would be playing the tournament on their home field later in the week. They'd won more than twenty games, a feat most people never expected. Why shouldn't they have a good night?

Yeah, playing the district tournament on their home field, the "million dollar field" is what everyone in the county called it. That much had been spent to construct this new site. Yet, after all the money poured into it, the place was mediocre at best. Water ponded at low spots in the outfield, and any water that did drain again stagnated along the first and third base areas. A soupy mixture made of red clay dirt covered parts of the coaches' boxes. So, the weather was appropriate as it made what should have been a memorable day just another dark time like the ones made of tears and anger and pain and lies that served as the ingredients of a high school career.

Moms and dads stepped onto a squishy field. The coach made no effort to improve the conditions of the arena that was the site for honoring their sons. The only night for special recognition was this one. The man had scheduled it for the last game of the season. If it washed out, no other night was available. That was so typical of this coach and his attitude toward this team. Standing on the infield grass, I wanted desperately to tell Dallas how proud of him I was. At the same time, I wanted to attack a thoughtless, lazy man who had the audacity to call himself a coach. Instead, I fought tears that welled in my eyes and thought of what might have been.

The ceremony was held quickly, and the sparse crowd settled in for the game. Players' disappointment was evident by the lethargic movements they made. What was usually a park filled with energetic high school fans turned out to be a place that echoed with the hollow sounds of folding chairs scraping on concrete as they were lined up behind the backstop, and heavy shoes clomped on aluminum bleachers. Even friends of these boys had abandoned them on what should have been a night for making memories.

What happened? How did things go so wrong? Was it just this one night, was it high school ball, or was the problem something that began fourteen years earlier. It's been said that during a crisis a man's life flashes before his eyes. Behind my soggy baby blues, the memories of my son's baseball playing days zipped by. The movie on my mind's screen wasn't a pleasant one, and I filled the role of villain in most scenes. If hell is real, then I've been there and returned, much like the old sailor in Coleridge's "Rhyme of the Ancient Mariner." My act of contrition is to write this story.

"He never made it as a baseball player, so he tried to get his son to make it for him."

RAY KINSELLA (KEVIN COSTNER), "FIELD OF DREAMS"

INTRODUCTION

You know that time of year. The earth begins to wake up from its winter slumber and begins to warm as if its blood were circulating for the first time in several months. That time of year is when dads like me go digging into piles of things stored in an outbuilding or a large closet. We surface with a "Ta-da," for we have uncovered the most important items for this time of year: bats, gloves, and baseballs.

The gloves are a bit stiff from having sat idly during the winter months, and the perspiration-soaked leather requires several hours of conditioning with lotions and oils and games of catch. Eventually, those gloves become pliable again and are in perfect condition for playing the game. The smell of a baseball glove sends most men tumbling back to their youth when they were members of formal teams or they met with groups of guys to play sandlot ball. What kind of team it is matters little to children; they play for the love of the game.

Only when we parents, dads especially, inject ourselves in baseball does the game become something different. An innocent, fun sport then becomes a political mess that even the United Nations can't untangle. Egos block the paths of a team's progress like rock slides across I-40 through the Smoky Mountains. Yes, dads' egos become the center of the attention. We all believe that our sons are big-league bound. Their great skills are evident to all but the most ignorant of people. Our sons must be on the field if the team has any hope of prevailing in games.

In order to massage individual egos and to ensure victory for the team, many of us dads coach. Most of us know little or nothing about the game, but we still coach to make sure our sons spend time between the lines instead of on the pine. Any man who has ever picked up a bat or glove considers himself an expert of the game. Some of us played only when we were children, so we find different avenues to baseball knowledge. As a high school teacher, I'd had the opportunity to talk with baseball coaches from several schools, and I'd also had the good fortune to discuss the game, practice activities, and game strategies with college and professional players and college and major league coaches. By the time I was asked to coach, my preparation was complete. I stepped onto the field sure that I was armed with the baseball knowledge that would deliver success to the members of my son's training league team. Yes, these six-year-old boys didn't realize how fortunate they were to have me as a coach. I could whip them into shape. What I lacked was the emotional maturity to coach my own son.

From the time that my son was four until he graduated from high school, I badgered him with baseball. He had to play. My twin brother's son had played and excelled, so Dallas' following in Brandon's footsteps was a must—to me. I don't know that I ever gave Dallas the opportunity to decide whether or not he wanted to play the game. I assumed that he did, mostly because I wanted him to play.

Through those years Dallas endured hours of torturous practice, more than his friends put in. I wanted to make sure that he was capable of playing with them. He cried when I fussed at him, he complained about the long hours of work, and he grimaced in pain when a ground ball took a bad hop and hit him in the chest or when the blisters on his hands from batting practice split and bled. Oh, but I was making a ball player out of him. I never considered what the price for all of this would be.

And I spent a small fortune on baseball over the years. He needed a new bat each season, and they ranged in price from $50 to $250. As his hands grew or his position in the field changed, new gloves were purchased. Hundreds of dollars poured from our checking account as we paid for membership on teams, bought uniforms, slept in motel rooms during weekend tournaments, fueled our cars, and fed ourselves. With that much money in the bank, I could have more wisely invested in Dallas' college education, but few men who are consumed with their sons' success think rationally when their children and sports are combined.

In the end, all of the money spent was actually wasted because Dallas rarely enjoyed playing baseball. He participated to please me. What those years of ball did was place undue pressure on our family, on each and every member. My wonderful wife and children lived in constant fear of my explosions over games, practice, or performance. In so many ways I was an abusive father who didn't realize that I was hurting my family. I thought that I was right and was making my son a better person. How much more deluded and wrong can a person be?

Worst of all, I came so dangerously close to destroying beyond repair the delicate relationship with my son. I pushed too hard; I fussed too much; I degraded too often. Fortunately, Dallas turned a blind eye to my actions and a deaf ear to my rantings. I became like his television or radio: when he had heard or seen enough, Dallas simply tuned me out. For that I am grateful.

This book is written for two purposes. First, it serves as a catharsis for me. The emotions which I encountered over the years, especially the negative ones, have gripped my soul as if I were possessed by some demon. Writing this is one way for me to face those demons and to exorcise them once and for all. My soul can be cleansed so that my remaining years won't be haunted with "what-ifs."

My second motivation for writing is that I know other dads must be suffering now as much as I suffered in those years. If they can see that someone else has been where they are now and has survived the turmoil, these men might have some hope. More important, if dads read about my journey through baseball hell with my son, maybe, just maybe, they won't stumble into the same pitfalls into which I fell face first. My intent is to prevent dads from becoming so blinded by their own egos that they fail to see what their sons want, what things are truly important to those children. Last, I hope that I can save the father-son relationships that might otherwise be destroyed by the perversion of the simple, wonderful game of baseball.

THE FAT KID IN RIGHT FIELD

I can't remember the year, but we neighborhood boys formed a softball team and, during our adolescent years, a baseball team to compete with three other teams from communities that bordered ours. Ball Camp had its share of good players, and we won plenty of games.

The games were played on a field located by Karns Elementary. Years later the field was demolished to make room for a new school. Coal was used to heat the old school, and the cinders from the used fuel had been dumped on the field and on the bank beside it. Boys wore shorts to play games because only the toughest gave a moment's thought to sliding into second or home plate. To

1

do so meant shredding the flesh that covered legs, and those jagged cuts healed slowly, even on the bodies of rough and tumble boys.

Our practice fields weren't much better. One was a cow pasture that was situated between the Wright's and the Robinson's houses. We met on there a couple of times a week. Ground balls took strange hops, and we dodged holes and cow manure when we chased after a ball skidding along the pasture grass. At other times, we practiced in a field beside Steve Harvey's house. It was another home for cows. That field was a about a mile from the house, but the Robinson's field was just down the road. Fat boys didn't like to ride bikes any farther than they had to ride, so my bother Jim and I preferred the closer field, although it was the rougher of the two.

Two men coached the team. Mr. Harry Wright was the main coach. Mr. Robinson assisted him. Mr. Wright gave much of his time to boys our age and served as the scoutmaster as well. The man constantly confused my twin and me, so when he hit a ball to either of us, he yelled,

"Your turn, Jim-Joe."

Mr. Wright was the man who filled out the line-ups. He was directly responsible for placing me in "baseball purgatory"—right field. Coach also set the batting order and made sure I remained the ninth batter for every game. He exiled me during games because he had watched me during practice. Mr. Wright knew that I faced certain physical danger if he placed me too close to the action. He also knew that my skills with the bat were nonexistent. He constantly yelled,

"You couldn't hit that one if you were standing on a stepladder!" This was a reference to pitches at eye level or higher that I inevitably attempted to crush. Still, he encouraged me in his own way to keep swinging and to keep my eye on the ball, something that I didn't really understand. Was I supposed to put my eye on a ball? Was I supposed to watch as the orb came buzzing across the plate or toward my head before it took a right turn into the strike zone?

Some fifty years later, I can remember most of the boys on that team. Ray Claiborne set up at first base. The boy could run so fast that he appeared to be flying. High school boys came to race him, but Ray won easily and walked back to the starting line to take on the next contender. One time he actually raced a small motorcycle, and maybe it was the only thing that beat him. During the games Ray never needed much of a hit to be on base. A nubber off the end of the bat was all he required to zip down the first base line. With any kind of help from the player who batted after him, Ray would score a run for our team. In high school he was a member of the relay teams that held school records for nearly twenty-five years. He took over his family's school bus operation, and he also built a putt-putt golf course. The boy had a knack for always landing on his feet like a cat, whether the situation included sports or business. Ironically, Ray struggled with his breathing after he developed a nasty craving for cigarettes. Fat boys like me were candidates to become smokers, but not guys like Ray. I never understood why he started the habit.

Steve Harvey played second base. He was a rather slender boy who wore glasses and looked rather professorial. To spectators he appeared fragile, but the boy was as tough as a pine knot. Steve also possessed ultimate grace, and he glided across the infield, scooped up balls, and threw runners out. For several years I lost contact with Steve, but I reconnected with him in a way as I taught his children in English classes. Still, I never saw their dad and suppose that was for the best, lest my memories of him wind up shattered if he'd changed during later life.

Larry Robinson played third base for the team. He wasn't a great player, but he occasionally knocked down a ball coming his way. He also produced a hit now and again. Larry played third because his dad was one of the coaches, and he was better than the rest of us scrubs on the team. He spent most of his time working on the small plot of land on which his family lived. Larry was killed in a car wreck the night of his junior prom. A missed curve on a rain-soaked road snuffed out his life in an instant as his car plowed head first into a relatively small, but sturdy and unforgiving tree.

Shortstop was manned by my childhood nemesis: Joey Wallace. God blessed Joey with athletic talent in every sport. He was stout, but not fat. His jet-black hair, that was cut so it parted perfectly, complimented his dark skin. His brown eyes only enhanced the good looks that drove girls to distraction. Joey looked like a young Elvis Presley. On the ball field his gifts became evident as he dove for hot grounders or backhanded balls out of other boys' range. Joey stabbed those balls, made acrobatic turns, and gunned out runners easily. He also possessed the power to send a hit over the opposing team's players. His hits cleared the bases and put our team in position to win. During his third grade year, his parents divorced, the first time our gang had ever heard of such a thing. That split seemed to steal some of his energy and childhood. His dad, Max, would appear at the door of our classroom and ask to speak to his son. Joey would walk out and return in just a few minutes. He always looked down as if the presence of his dad embarrassed him, especially since we all knew what was going on at his house. I saw Joey maybe fifteen years ago. He worked at a window manufacturer. After all those years, he still had the good looks, but I'm not so sure that life had been kind to him as an adult.

Our pitcher most years was Pat Wright. Pat was a wiry kid, and he was tougher than a piece of pig iron. His hair was an almost orange color, and eyebrows matched. His thin lip seldom parted to allow many words out. Pat stayed sunburned most of the summer, the plight of fair skinned redheads. He could play any position, but his ability to pitch strikes and keep our team in the game was his most valuable asset, that and his hitting ability. Pat could also hit the long ball, and although he wasn't as fast as Ray Claiborne, Pat managed to squeeze extra bases from singles. During his early adult life, Pat was a carpenter who enjoyed smoking marijuana. In fact, he is the first person I ever saw using the stuff. On that night he and his new group of friends huddled around the back stoop of our house and passed a joint around. The way Pat and others fell to their hands and knees to retrieve a dropped "roach" from the tall blades of grass in our back yard convinced me to not to ever take a hit. I was purer than Bill Clinton because I never even took any smoke from a joint into my mouth, not to mention my lungs. Pat died not too many years ago from cancer. I wish I had seen him more as we grew up, but he lived outside Knoxville on a farm he had bought and was happy with his life and I was busy with mine.

Our catcher was Clebert Roberts. A dark-skinned boy with brown hair that bleached in the summer sun, he donned the equipment that only provided minimal protection. On numerous occasions games stopped until the stinging pain to a body part hit by a foul ball subsided and crying eyes could be wiped dry with the sleeve of a dirt-covered T-shirt. Clebert was courageous to crouch behind the plate and attempt to catch fastballs and curve balls. He was a scrappy boy who was only an average player. After high school he joined the Marines, and then he exploded physically. What had once been a skinny body became a gigantic frame of over six feet, and his weight edged over two hundred pounds. Clebert played football on the Marine team. His dad was hard on him when he was a child. If the boy were beaten in a fight, and back then it was a sure bet that he would lose every encounter, his dad dragged him back outside for round two, and the results were the same as the first. Clebert was named after his dad, but he changed his name in later years to Robbie. I suppose he did so as way to throw a slap at a father who was so cruel to him and to distance himself a little farther from the man.

Our ace pitcher was Donny Brewer. Rumors circulated that he was too old to play on our team, but no one ever questioned him or demanded to see a birth certificate that would prove his age. What Donny gave us was a chance to win every game. He threw hard fastballs. During his wind-up, he kept the ball hidden until it exploded from his hand and barreled toward home plate. He also was a bit wild. I never figured out if he was naturally that way or if it was a part of his pitching style. In most games he plunked a couple of boys on opposing teams. At that age, whether they cried or toughed out the pain was a fifty-fifty bet. The effects of those hit batters carried through the game. Boys scooted off the plate a little more, and if Donny threw a curve ball that appeared to be heading for a body part, they bailed out of the box and settled for a called strike. Woe unto a batter that got a hit against Donny because the next time up he would be standing on first wearing a red circle with two sets of stitches, the perfect impression of a baseball on his back, arm, or butt.

Pay backs are hell, and the guys on our team knew that whoever batted the inning after Donny hit a player was going to get tagged. It was an unwritten rule of the game, and although none of us looked forward to the pain, we knew it was nothing personal.

Not long ago I ran into Donny's sister-in-law. She told me that he'd died soon after her husband, and his older brother, had passed.

My twin brother Jim played left field. He caught the ball pretty well, and his throws were strong, but sometimes off target. He was a heavy child until he struggled through a bout of hepatitis that knocked thirty pounds from his frame. Every once in a while, Jim played on the infield. He wasn't a horrendous player, but he was slow of foot enough to make him a second late getting to the ball. In the outfield he felt more comfortable and helped the team more. His bat wasn't the strongest part of his game. He muscled some balls for hits, but too many times either he left home plate with the ball slowly rolling toward an infielder or after the umpired had called strike three.

Donny Turpin played center field on the team. I don't remember anything about him and haven't seen him the last forty years. He must have possessed some speed to have been put in center, but I can't swear to that. It's sad to think that some boys with whom I spent so much time I no longer can recall.

I was stationed in right field. A round-bellied, skinny-legged child, I was placed in that position throughout my entire softball and baseball playing days. Back then, every team exiled the absolute worst player to right field. I was poor at judging fly balls, and if one were hit over my head, my fat body couldn't waddle fast enough to run it down. Ground balls often rolled between my legs. Our right field had only sparse clumps of grass, and balls often careened off them and scooted in weird angles that were in the opposite direction of where I was heading. Sometimes they shot off the clumps and zapped my shins or stomach. Behind the red clay dirt outfield was a short road covered with loose gravel and tar. On the opposite side of the road a chain-link fence that encircled the high school football stadium was anchored. My sole job was to chase down all the balls that everyone knew would be hit over my head or between my legs and throw them back in. To add insult to injury, my arm strength was inadequate to make the throw all the way back to the infield, so another player met me half way, not serving as a cut-off man, but to return the ball to the pitcher. By the time I reached the ball, the batters scored, based cleared, and opposing players sat on the bench and waited for the game to begin again.

My own teammates swore at me and made comments about my inability to play. They made those comments loud enough for everyone around the field to hear. So, I was not only humiliated by my failures to make plays, but was also brutalized by the comments of those who were supposed to be my friends. Looking back, I can understand why they were so cruel. Losing sucked even then, and it was worse when some fat kid in right field gave away runs.

The coach always told me that I was being placed in right field because I was left handed and would be able to catch fly balls hit to that side. I watched the action of the game from my vantage point far removed from participation, and I grew curious as to what playing first base was like. As a left-hander I could catch the ball and could guard the line I told myself. I begged the coach to let me play one inning at that position, but during the entire time of playing ball as a kid, I never was given the opportunity to field a ground ball or catch a throw made on the infield. I was permanently banished to the nether regions of right field.

Unbelievable but true, my ability at the plate was more limited. I stood at the plate prepared to knock the ball out of the park, but as soon as the pitcher released the ball, my feet shuffled and my body moved away from home plate. If a boy threw a curve, I bailed out of the box. Most of the time, I never saw the ball at all. I either pulled my head around as I swung or closed my eyes. I desperately wanted to hit the ball, but the sad fact was that I was terrified of it and of being beaned by it.

In such a manner I spent my childhood baseball playing days. Always being too fat, too slow, too unskilled, or too scared kept me from becoming anything better than horrible as a player. Unknown to all, including me, during those difficult times the fate of my future son Dallas was sealed as a baseball player.

Spending those years of my life so thoroughly embarrassed and humiliated, I promised myself that no son of mine would ever experience the same things.

My dad was a good man, but he played ball with us only one time. He accidentally hit my older brother with the ball on that occasion, and he dropped the ball, walked into the house, and never played again. On the day that Dallas was born, I vowed to work with him on his playing abilities so that he would have good memories of his youth and of ball. Most of all, I wanted my son to be a player who could hold his own with other kids and, yes, one about whom I could say, "That's my boy."

Unfortunately, my over-involvement, harshness, and demands might have been every bit as defeating for Dallas as my dad's failure to play at all was for me. So begins the story of a father, a son, and a game. In this case, however, the combination is one that led to unhappy times and suffering of both persons for most of fourteen years.

MY SON

On February 4, 1985, my life was forever changed, and for the baby boy who arrived, life sometimes would be something more strenuous than it should be. Joseph Dallas Rector is my son's name. He carries Joseph, the name of my wife's dad and my name as well. Dallas is my dad and brother's name. The boy never had a chance with me as his dad.

Two things were instantly noticeable at birth. First was the hooked, bulbous nose that was a physical characteristic of the Rector clan. The other features were his eyes. They were a green, but not a brilliant color. Instead, they appeared almost olive in color with flecks of brown. Those eyes looked passed a person to his insides. Eyes such as those show all that the boy feels in his heart. Throughout the years, those eyes burned holes into my soul as they questioned why I had so mistreated their owner.

We brought Dallas home, and he completed our family. Lacey, his sister, was three and a half years older. Upon our entering the house, she sat on the couch, and we placed her brother in her arms. A bond was instantly formed, and for their lives they have remained close. She would soon enough be the first child to experience the over involvement and weighty demands of her father.

When Lacey turned six, I signed her up for tee ball. She was a cute, pudgy little girl with a sweetness for which all dads pray. Lacey also was strong. She could hit the ball better than many of the boys on the team. Inability to catch a fly ball, stop a grounder, or throw straight overshadowed her hitting prowess. I worked with her, but Lacey had a stubborn streak. When my demands sounded more like orders from a drill instructor, she quit. That's it; she simply refused to do any more. No amount of fussing or complaining changed her. She'd had enough.

On one occasion, I persuaded her to keep working by letting her hit. I pitched to her, and she hit a few grounders. Then, one pitch that was straight down the pike met the wood of her bat, and before I could move, the baseball caught me squarely in the groin. I dropped like a rock to the ground and writhed in pain. My precious daughter came skipping to me with a huge smile on her face. She asked if I was OK and then stated that she'd hit the ball just like I'd taught her. Lacey turned her back and skipped back the house where she happily played for the rest of the day.

One of the first errands I ran after Dallas' arrival took me to the local Walmart. I purchased a ball glove, a cheap one, but one that would be my son's first. I kept it tucked away until Dallas was old enough and strong enough to place the thing on his hand. I excitedly waited for the day to come, and when it did, I'd present the glove to him. He would smell the leather of the glove and of the baseball and instantly fall in love with it and that game, just as I had done when I was a boy. That smell would be forever etched in his memory, and a flood of memories about baseball, friends, family, and spring would come flooding in his years as an adult. Too bad they would all be bad ones.

Dallas was unlike any boy I had ever encountered. He loved to wrestle in the floor with his dad when he was no more than a couple of years old. I put him on his tricycle for the first time when he was no more than a year and a half old. He showed not one ounce of fear. Dallas would shoot basketballs at the small goal hanging on his closet door for hours. I was overjoyed for he seemed to love sports above all else. One of his favorite games as a toddler was to put his forehead on the carpet and to zip across it on his hands and knees so fast that it left a carpet burn. He led with his head, and for that reason, his entire life as a small child was marked with stitches and bandages on his forehead.

When Dallas grew a bit older, other things vied for his attention. He played in his bedroom floor for hours with cars and trucks. Dallas made the sounds for his vehicle, and he created a world in which they were used. The boy loved to have his mother read to him, and he'd crawl upon her lap and hand her a stack of books. He listened as Amy read each of them and drifted off into make-believe worlds that books sparked.

Dallas possessed an analytical mind as a child. His two favorite things to play with were Legos and jigsaw puzzles. For hours he sat at a table or in the floor; he constructed buildings or fit puzzle pieces into their proper places with ease. I couldn't understand the fascination because doing things such as those meant having to sit still.

Through the years so many activities competed with baseball. Dallas enjoyed paintball. He bought guns, rounds, and protective equipment with money he received as birthday and Christmas gifts. With friends Josh Bremseth and William Hayes, Dallas spent adventurous hours running through wooded areas close to the house in pursuit of an enemy so that he could pelt him with paint bullets.

The boy's greatest love was video games. Over the years he bought and sold several different game systems: PlayStations, an Xbox, and Nintendo. Games became standard gifts at Christmases and birthdays. For hours Dallas holed up in his room and played them. During the summers he stayed up until early morning and slept until midday. He would have been happy to have never stepped outside. His only exercise was what his thumbs got as he expertly handled the controls.

I grumbled and growled about what I perceived to be his laziness, and on plenty of occasions I fussed at him and told him to go outside and play like kids were supposed to do. That was true twenty-five years earlier, but his generation gave up playing and adopted couch potato games instead.

Dallas inherited a genetic defect—a terrible overbite, much like the one I had as a child. At the age of eleven he experienced the suffering that accompanies having braces that look like railroad tracks running across his teeth. I told him how fortunate he was to have them to correct his out of whack teeth, but nothing sucks the confidence out of a boy like wearing them for three years or more. Dallas quit smiling during the braces years, and it would take him until his mid-twenties to allow a warm, loving smile to take over his face again.

To make matters worse, Dallas had also been given the same build as his dad. My entire family sported love "handles." That's the collections of weight that settle above the hipbones of some unfortunate people. Dallas was so ashamed of his body's appearance that he refused to take off his shirt in public throughout high school. He was so shaken that he quit basketball after one season because the jersey he wore showed too much of him. Added to that was a growing stomach from too much junk food and too little exercise. Before he knew what had hit, the boy was rounding out in the middle and wouldn't lose the weight until puberty performed its magic.

School and a poor self-image wreaked havoc on Dallas. His confidence was bottomed out, and he allowed it to affect his grades. Dallas had been the favorite of the entire day care that he attended. In fact, the teachers and assistants cried on his last day. I took him to kindergarten at Ball Camp, and from the first day of school in August until the following April, I left him sitting in the gym and crying in pure misery. His teacher told the class that she hated them and couldn't stand little boys, and she spent each day crying herself. Such an introduction led to years of his despising school and all that was associated with it. He'd fallen from the good graces of day care into the swarthy pit of hatefulness of an incompetent public school teacher's room.

In middle school Dallas' grades were fair to poor. He gave little effort, and when I asked him about school, he lied and told me, "Things are fine. I'm doing well in all my classes." Report cards told a different story, and the more I pressed him, the worse he did. I had always told him that I expected 100% effort. If he gave that, I would never demand more of him. However, he fought with me, and our battles became more heated. He didn't believe what I said because my actions on so many occasions proved my words to be a lie. To be honest, I wanted my son to be a wonderful student. I was fearful that any poor achievement instantly would reflect upon me as a father and as a teacher. It wasn't easy to push other kids to excellence when my own fell short of the mark.

We both recall the battles over spelling words. I would walk to his room to quiz him on them, he'd misspell the majority, and I'd run him through the ringer for an hour as I force-fed him the correct spelling and meanings. It was the same thing week in and week out, and neither of us ever tried a different approach to the problem.

By high school Dallas had gained a bit more self-confidence. Suddenly, he became a good student, and grades were never an issue again. Dallas also began to enjoy school activities. His senior class voted him "Most School Spirited," the highest honor he believed his classmates could have bestowed upon him. He also had scads of friends, and they enjoyed themselves in a variety of activities.

Dallas swallowed his pain. When he was just a child and I would spank him, he refused to cry until I left his room. We fought our battles over rules at home, schoolwork, proper behavior, and a thousand other irrelevant points. During any confrontation, Dallas fought only for so long. Then he stopped, became quiet, and shut down. He internalized all the anger and frustration that he felt. Dallas refused to let it escape. Instead, he became a meek, almost mousy person who simply allowed others to run roughshod over him. Tragedies only caused him to close ranks more tightly. He told people what they wanted to hear, not what he truly felt or believed. I used to think others intimidated Dallas, but I often wondered if he weren't really controlling situations by deciding how each person would behave through his lack of involvement.

For most of his teen years fear dictated Dallas' life. He had so much to worry about for a kid so young. Most of all, Dallas didn't want to fail, not for himself and for me. He couldn't take the disappointment that I showed when he didn't meet my expectations. The proof of this is best shown in the following point.

My wife, Amy, and I came across a good deal on a small car. The mileage was high, but the owner had taken good care of the car. Its one drawback was the manual transmission. Still, we bought the car for Dallas' fifteenth birthday. I would teach him to drive this car after he got his learner's permit. Dallas promised me that he was studying faithfully so that he could pass the written examination portion of the driver's exam. I took a half-day off work on his birthday and drove him to the testing center. The entire trip to the testing site, Dallas was silent. I asked him if he was nervous, and he assured me that he wasn't. He walked in and was directed to the testing area, and I sat in the waiting room. I was excited about this day, and I thought he was too. However, when he finished his test, he came to me and said, "I failed. I'm sorry." The truth was that Dallas had given no more than an occasional glance to the driver's manual. He believed that he could fake it like he'd done so many times before, but nothing other than studying would help him to pass this test.

Immediately, I was livid, and the entire trip back to school I yelled and ranted about how he had let himself down. I made sure he knew that the gift we had bought him wasn't so special since he couldn't drive. I made him feel worse than he must have already felt. My rage erupted partly due to embarrassment. How would I explain Dallas' failure to his mother, uncles, aunts, and my friends, and students?

I told Dallas to let me know when he had really done some studying for the test. Only then would I take him for another chance. That was in February, and by May I was growing more and more agitated with my son. We had driven through the local industrial park enough that Dallas had become an expert driver of a manual transmission. I finally gave him and ultimatum at May's end. "You have until the end of the second week of June to take your driver's test and pass it. If you don't, you won't be allowed to go anywhere or do anything outside of playing baseball."

I don't regret that statement. I knew that Dallas wanted to have his permit. What I didn't realize was that he was afraid to take the test again because he didn't want to fail again and disappoint me. He would rather not drive than have the pressure to succeed. That's the way he always thought about things where I was concerned.

It's amazing that Dallas has survived through the years. I've been a taskmaster who has steadily eroded his confidence. In spite of me, Joseph Dallas Rector has become a wonderful, lovable, and caring person. The good Lord has surely watched over him and protected him from the rants and raves of a father who meant well but just didn't understand what he was doing to the son he loved more than his own life.

BASEBALL 101

I nervously drove to the ball field as my five-year-old son rode with me as co-pilot. He was oblivious to the serious nature of the situation. This trip was his first practice as the member on an organized baseball team. At five, he began his ball career, and I wanted to make sure that he performed in spectacular fashion. That way he would impress the coaches enough to put him in a position on the infield. Just as has always been the case, at that age, being relegated to the outfield meant that the kid had little, if any, ability. He was tagged for the rest of his baseball career as *community league player.* No, I wouldn't allow him to suffer in the outfield the way that I had.

Dallas and I had practiced for at least a year before he was old enough to join a team. Yes, he was four, and even younger, when the practice sessions began. I forced him outside in freezing temperatures in early March and continued the trips through the scalding months of summer and the muggy, stifling months of early fall. We had to practice. I subjected my son to drills that seemed too demanding for any young person who wanted to play the game.

"Put the lid on the pot. Keep your tailgate down. Don't flip your glove. Come get the ball; don't wait for it to play you."

I barked those phrases to a child who had been walking on steady feet for two and a half, maybe three years. Already I pushed him to be the best.

Dallas worked hard at the baseball drills. Sometimes he had no idea what I was talking about, but he tried to get the ground ball, catch the fly ball, and make the throw. He wanted to please me. A word of praise was good enough to keep his attention for another fifteen minutes.

Hey, I wasn't smart enough to know that. Instead of praise, I fussed at him. I told him he wasn't giving one hundred percent. I frowned, and my curt words displayed my displeasure while having no idea that they cut to the quick of his little heart. I had watched my twin brother work his son Brandon and believed that his way was the best one to teach Dallas. It had to be because Brandon developed into such a talented player. I dismissed the thought that natural ability had anything to do with it. Enough hard work and effort could overcome any shortfall of talent.

So, after a year's practice, he and I were on our way to his first meeting with a team. I had dreamed about this day for more years that my son had been alive. Dallas, on the other hand, seemed totally unaffected by the situation. To him, the day was to be one where he played with other boys and had fun. Fun! Ha! He had a job to do, and I hoped that adequate preparation had him ready for it.

That early spring afternoon was unusually warm. Dallas wore a pair of sweat pants, a T-shirt, and his new baseball cleats. His glove was the smallest that stores sold, yet it swallowed his hand and most of his wrist. Dallas' work with it over the last months allowed him to feel comfortable. He wore a baseball cap that had the perfect curvature to the bill. I not only wanted my son to react like baseball player, but I also wanted him to look like one. A perfectly sculpted bill of his cap announced to all that here was a boy who could "walk the walk and talk the talk." I told him part of being a good ball player was looking like one, and my little boy certainly looked every bit the baseball player that day.

The two coaches met with parents and boys in an open field beside an elementary school. They explained how boys would be placed in positions. Just as I expected, they would put the best players at key positions; others would be scattered throughout the outfield so they didn't get in the way of the game. Two lines formed, and boys paired up to throw and then to field ground balls. The coaches watched with critical eyes each of the boys of the team. Sometimes a smile or the shake of a head would flash quickly between the coaches, something that indicated that a particular boy had ability. At other times the coaches stood frozen in position as they watched with horrified faces the boy who couldn't throw or catch. Clipboards held papers with players' names, and on these the two men scribbled comments.

I stayed out of the action until one coach asked me to watch over part of the group. He'd done so because we attended the same high school, me graduating three years before him. I stepped in excitedly. Before long, I was showing a boy how to throw the ball by releasing it and pointing with his throwing hand at the glove of his partner. I instructed another boy to keep his tailgate down when the ground ball came his way. All the while I kept an eye on Dallas, and if he talked, smiled, or goofed-off, I barked at him, "Get serious about what you're doing. You play like you practice." He looked at me with hurt and embarrassment washing over his soul and into his eyes, but I wasn't interested in that. I wanted Dallas to perform well, period.

The practice ended, and on the way home, I chewed on my five-year-old son for not giving his best at practice. He sat quietly in the car seat beside me. He uttered not a single word. By the time we reached home, he seemed to be all right, but his quietness remained. I told him that he would have another chance at the next practice. That one would be on the ball field, and there he could show his best stuff. He nodded his head and went to his room. That night he played with his trucks, looked at a couple of books, and shot basketball at the goal on his closet door. Dallas had banished baseball to the farthest recesses of his mind. It was the first of many times that the boy left baseball on the outside of his bedroom door.

I worried about Dallas' status on the team. He worked to be a second baseman like his cousin Brandon, but only the coaches' decision would determine his fate. At the next practice the boys gathered around the coaches for instructions and field positions. Standing along the left field fence, my heart raced as each boy left the huddle and sprinted to his new place. The head coach looked at Dallas, said something to him, and sent him on his way. When he reached third base, Dallas stopped, looked at me with a grin, and waved. It wasn't second base, but he made the infield. The hot corner was his first baseball position.

John Alred, the head coach, asked me to catch throws made to home plate from the players, and I jumped at the chance to do so. During infield practice, I asked him why Dallas had been assigned to third. He never looked at me as he began to answer,

"He's got one of the best gloves on this team. He won't let many balls get past him. His size keeps his range from being good, but at third he doesn't have to move much."

I tried to control the beaming smile that tried so desperately to escape my lips.

"John, can Dallas make that throw from third to first?"

"Nope," John said. "All he has to do is stop the ball and get it back to the pitcher's circle. If we hold hitters to singles, we'll be OK."

With that the season began. I had been drafted by the two coaches to catch behind the plate during our team's turn to bat. There I constantly ran my mouth as I told players how to stand, swing, and follow through. My jabbering became more intense when Dallas took his turn. I corrected every move that he made; it's a wonder he made contact with the ball at all. But he did hit some balls, and he got his share of singles.

During the games I felt sorry for John's son. Matthew was a gigantic kid for this age group. He played first base and batted in the top of the order. John was a high school athlete who excelled. He went on to play college football. Matthew didn't inherit all of John's abilities, and the major thing he lacked was John's intensity. His personality was one that was more reserved, like his mother's. During the games, John was brutal to Matthew. Any mistake that occurred on the field in some way was the boy's fault. John berated him, and many were the games when Matthew finished out an inning or an at-bat with tears streaming down his face. I used to talk to my wife Amy about how rough John was on his son, not at all recognizing the same flaw in my own character. It was one of those instances when the "pot called the kettle black."

That year Dallas learned much about the game. John and Joey Crawford, the other coach, were excellent teachers and patient men with boys other than their own sons. We won more games than we lost, but we didn't bring home the championship trophy. Dallas had me to put up with at every game, but somehow he managed to survive the season. With twenty-twenty hindsight, I now see that the best part of the contest to him was the free drink he received from the concession stand at each game's end. He showed more speed running up the long hill to snag a suicide coke than he ever showed on the field. I also remember the look on his face when he received his first-ever team trophy. He glowed with pride, and he brought it to me to make sure that I approved of it. I patted him on the shoulder and told him to just wait until next year. Then we'd win the league and he'd receive a better trophy. Dallas placed his memento on a chair and walked to the other boy, his head bowed just slightly. Again, I had tried to encourage him with a sucker punch.

Sometimes bits of humor crept into our world of baseball. One of the funniest moments came during a game in the middle of the season. Dallas didn't make time to use the portable restrooms before the game. I suppose he was afraid that I'd squall at him for missing warm-ups. He held on until the third inning. Then he came to me to whisper,

"Dad, I have to pee."

I barked back, "You should have taken care of that before the game started!"

Dallas countered,

"I know, but I REALLY have to go, bad!"

By then I was in a huff with him for not taking care of the matter earlier. I was irate with a five-year-old boy for not using the bathroom, and I grumbled to him,

"The only place I know that you can go is behind the dugout."

My comment was meant as a joke because the back of the dugout was in plain view of the field behind ours. Dallas, however, took me at my word, left the dugout, and leaned against the wall as he relieved himself. Something about little boys makes them urinate in high arches, and Dallas was no exception.

I heard the laughter from the parents, and then somebody in the dugout yelled,

"Dallas is pissing in front of everybody!"

I jumped from my seat and hurried to the doorway, where I met my son coming back to the team. He smiled at me and said,

"Whew! I just about didn't make it."

As team catcher, I also argued with other coaches. One man in particular infuriated me. He was a young dad with reddish-blonde hair that was thinner than mine. He was cocky, and the guy continually bumped his gums to the distraction of our players. My own shortcomings were always annoying most when they appeared in others. During one instance I called him out about his mouth, and he and I ended up nose-to-nose and toes-to-toes. Others separated us before any fighting could break out. Dallas watched in horror as his dad came close to brawling at a little league game. It was just another occasion when his dad acted more like the child than the son did.

The worst thing about this league was that the seasons were over by the time the end of school arrived the first of June. No more baseball to play for the rest of the summer seemed impossible. I took advantage of the lull to practice Dallas in all phases of his game—hitting, fielding, and catching. Usually, we went to the baseball field in the middle of the day. I worked this five-year-old boy until he nearly dropped. His face burned red from exhaustion and heat, and his hair dripped with sweat. When we finished the torture, I stopped to buy him a drink, in my mind some kind of reward from a benevolent father, but the entire ride home I spent complaining about something he had done incorrectly or about his lack of hustle. Dallas would continue to practice ball because I wanted him to do so, not because he did. He'd much rather have played in his room, read a book, or watched television. The best way to summarize the season is to say that Dallas' dad was one giant asshole.

LITTLE LEAGUE POLITICS

Most father and son duos enter baseball leagues with a naïve view of what's going on. Kids are excited to play a game with friends. They don't care if the team is competitive or if it can't line up. These little guys are much more excited about new ball equipment, uniforms, and concession stands than about wins and losses. On the other hand, some dads want their sons, and occasionally, daughters, on competitive teams. Wins and losses do matter to them; otherwise, they ask, why is the score kept? What most folks don't realize is that community ball leagues are fraught with politics, and only those who are most skillful in dealing with them will be successful.

Officers are elected for leagues. The candidates are dads who choose to immerse themselves in every aspect of the league. While some officers are hesitant candidates, others crisscross the playing fields as their campaigns reach the dugouts of every coach. Slaps on the back are given, jokes are told, and *pie-in-the-sky* promises are made in order to secure a wining tally of votes.

Most people want to know what is so important about the presidency of a Little League. The answer is *POWER*. Many of the men who would be president are individuals who long to have control over others. Some have lousy lives and jobs where they are subordinates. Someone always tells them what to do, when to do it, and how it should be done. Their chances for being the leaders of anything come at three places: home, church, and little league. At home the dad can be an overly demanding person whose swagger is due to his ability to lord over his wife, children, and the family pet. At church a man has the opportunity to serve on its board. There he can help develop a large budget and make decisions as to how the money is spent. In youth sporting leagues, a dad can have a say-so in every facet of the operation. Sure, some men serve because they love the game or kids, but they are exceptions.

Most presidents also coach a team in the league. They have power over scheduling and work on the match-ups for the season. Additionally, they schedule fields and batting cages for practices. On more than one occasion teams that I coached received terrible times for practices. Saturday afternoons at 2:00 p.m. don't bring out kids for practice. Parents are jealous of their free time and would rather enjoy other activities on the weekend. So, half the team practiced and the other half spent the afternoon in such wasteful activities as swimming, hiking, or taking in a movie.

The president of the league usually knows which teams will be the strong ones for a particular season. If he wishes, he can stack the schedule so that those teams consistently play the late games, or he can have a good team play consecutive nights before his team faces them in an upcoming game. It's been done! These guys find plenty of ways to give their teams edges while they are handicapping others.

The league is highly selective about its coaches. That I was asked to coach surprised me. My twin brother had coached in the league previously, and he had gone several rowdy rounds with the powers-that-be. The collection of coaches was like a fraternity, something of which I wanted no part. I viewed their cliquish ways as juvenile and detrimental to the quality of the league. Once a man was chosen as a coach, he was required to take part in all sorts of activities. On early spring Saturdays before the season began, coaches gathered to complete field maintenance. We dug trenches to drain water, edged infields, moved stands, strung temporary fences, and picked up trash. The league demanded this intensive work of its coaches several times during the season.

Coaches were also expected to complete field maintenance before and after ballgames. If a team played the 5:00 game, the coaches were to arrive early enough to line the field, bring out all equipment, and make sure garbage cans were empty. Coaches of the late games again picked up trash, pulled the bases, and dragged the field, usually with their own vehicles. The demands on the coaches were too much. Many of these dads worked until 5:00, and they simply couldn't arrive in time to take care of these chores. After-game work kept a youngster waiting for too long as his dad completed his duties. Any time coaches complained about time constraints, the president and his cohorts told them to *deal with it or quit coaching*. They cared more about field maintenance than about keeping quality coaches.

The league always needed to raise money, and candy sales came around with each season. Each boy was expected to sell at least twenty one-dollar candy bars. A photographer who was part of the governing body contracted with the league to take individual and team pictures. A portion of the charges was returned to the league. Concession stands raised small fortunes for the association. A small fountain drink cost patrons fifty cents, and the profit from each sale was no less than forty cents. Even in those days, a season's income from the stand must have averaged $35,000. What made this money-raising so perplexing was the decree that teams had to find their own sponsors, whose names were placed on T-shirts printed by a business contracted by the league. Few folks realized that all of this money came in addition to the fees that each child paid to play in the league. Easily the officers and league must have handled moneys amounting to nearly $100,000 each year.

To cut costs, the league didn't hire umpires for games in the lower levels. Teams with children ages five through eight played games with other coaches as officials. Most of the time these men did their best to call games fairly. Still, parents harassed them unmercifully and sometimes challenged them either verbally or physically. Some coaches carried grudges from previous games, and others looked for a competitive advantage. These men took every opportunity to make calls against their closest rivals. Of course, that led to more heated words and battles, all because the league was too cheap to pay high school kids $5 to call a game.

The ballpark was locked each night. No one was allowed on the fields except during the designated times. Offenders were dealt with harshly. A father and son who wanted to improve the child's skills needed to climb the fences to sneak on the diamonds. If a league official caught trespassing fathers and sons, he might contact law enforcement, or the child could be booted from the league. Only the mere pleasure of the governing board could save those who dared violate the rules.

The board also chose the coaches for the all-star teams. The decision was based on who patronized these men, not on which persons could best lead the select team to victories in tournaments. Too, coaches' sons were automatically put on these special teams. Some of those boys weren't the best players on their teams, let alone of all-star quality. Of course, the coaches who had been hand-selected by the officers determined playing times. A father who was not in the favor of the president could expect precious little playing time for his son in tournaments. Even if the boy's talents could lift the team to victory, his fate was to ride the bench until the rules declared that he had to play. Yes, grown men used little boys as ways to strike back at their enemies.

Not a single president ever wanted to hear about changes. They decided what was best for the kids, and then they closed their ears. In our area, only one other community played Little League ball. The rules included no stealing bases until the ball crossed the plate and no balking by pitchers. Other community organizations converted to AABC rules, what most of us know as *real* baseball. Dads who wanted their sons to participate in this kind of program petitioned the board about changing, but to no avail. The officials stated that they wanted to do what was best for the children. It's amusing that such a statement is made in the face of so many baseball leagues abandoning Little League in favor of the AABC organization. After years of trying to work from within the system, dads withdrew their sons from this program and tried to find spots within baseball leagues in other communities. If the child had talent and ambition to play base-ball in later years, searching out new places to play was the only hope.

The game of baseball is a simple one. It requires a piece of ground for a field and only minimum equipment. The game loses its simplicity when grown-ups, yes, people like me, dads who become coaches and league officers, involve themselves. Maybe the game is purer and more fun when boys find a sandlot on which to hold their games. The only politics on those fields occur when boys lobby captains to pick them first. Yes, adding an adult instantly complicates and confounds.

THE SEASON OF CHAMPIONS

I answered the phone, and the man with whom I had nearly come to blows the previous year was on the other end. This is the way the second baseball season began.

Billy Hayes called to ask me if I would be interested in coaching with him for the coming season. I didn't know the man, nor did I realize the he and I crossed paths the year before. Neither was Billy aware that I was a dad he was ready to knock out. What we did know was that our sons had developed a friendship in kindergarten and that they would enjoy playing together. So, when Billy asked me if I would be interested in helping, I accepted.

Each of us brought strengths to this alliance. Billy had a memory like no other person whom I knew. He could recall every single detail of any ball game in which his son William played. I couldn't remember what happened in a game the day after it was over. Billy also knew the boys in the league, an invaluable tool when draft day came. He managed to pick a group of boys who were good ball players or who had potential to be good. Of course, in draft ball, some of the players had little or no skills, and all teams had to take their share of those boys. Those we would have to work with before the season began.

I had a different specialty. I knew baseball. Being around my brother and his son and having made friends with the high school baseball coach aided me in learning the intricacies of the sport. I had picked their brains for practice drills. I had paid close attention to the instruction they gave to boys about batting. I asked them the proper mechanics of pitching. My contribution to this team would come before games were played.

I acted as a taskmaster. I worked with each infielder to correct flaws he might have in fielding a ground ball. William played second base, and Dallas filled the shortstop position. Zach Fine, Bobby Berry, Drew Shockley, and Travis McCown rounded out a solid platoon for the infield. I hit sharp ground balls to these boys. They needed to get rid of any fears of the ball that might cause them to make a mistake. Sometimes the ball took a bad hop and hit boys in the stomach, shoulder, leg, or face. I would check an injured boy to make certain that he suffered only a momentary pain. However, if Dallas were the one hurt, I told him to "walk it off," and then I would hit him another ball immediately so that he didn't ever have the time to become gun shy.

I also served as the pitcher when our team batted. Other coaches tossed the ball in an arc as if the boys were playing softball. Some of the big boys on those teams hit home runs as they swung up under the ball, but I knew that their troubles would begin in another year or two when they no longer could hit anything but pop-ups by swinging in such a way. Even though my pitches came in underhanded, I threw the ball flat and fast. Our boys worked on hitting the ball that way. Sometimes they struck out, but most of the time the players put the ball into play. During games, coaches could stand in the field with their teams. I always stood where I could yell instructions to the infield. My constant reminders made nervous wrecks of boys who listened to me. Dallas was one of them. On several occasions he made a mistake because he paid too much attention to me and not enough to the ball. Then I would growl at him for making the mistake. His head would fall, his chin touching his sternum. I looked at him with devilish eyes and quipped,

"Get your head up! Do it right!"

With other players I was kinder, but not much. William was a born out-fielder, and he would play that position well during his high school years. Zach was positioned at third, but he had a tendency to go after the ball, regardless of where it was hit. Numerous times he would sprint from third base to the right of second in pursuit of a ball. That another player was ready to make the play was irrelevant to Zach. Travis was a quiet child who caught most every ball thrown to him at first base, something that doesn't happen much in training league. Drew Shockley proved to be our ace in the hole. He played the pitcher position. There a boy would stand in a large circle around what would have been a pitching mound. Drew zipped quickly to the ball, so much so that, unlike Zach, we told him to get to the ball any time that he could. Drew made several spectacular plays that season.

When the team batted, I coached the first base side, and Billy coached third base. We continued that set up throughout our coaching association that lasted for twelve years. My constant chatter and instructions to the boys as they batted began to annoy them and Billy. He finally told me not to talk to the boys so much. I went out the next inning and, without realizing, began to jabber away again. When Dallas took his place at the plate, I went over every thing that he should be doing. He hit the ball, but not as hard as I thought he should have hit. When he reached first base, I was waiting to chastise him for whatever he had done incorrectly. He dreaded being stuck there. In fact, he would rather have struck out than to have stood on first base and listen to me.

Our major rivalry was with a team coached by Jim Butler and Greg Morrow. Jim I had always liked, but Greg rubbed me the wrong way. Later when he was league president, I didn't trust him to carry through with what he promised. Too, his son, a year older than our boys, was monstrous and could park the ball across the fence. We battled during the season, and at the end of the year, our teams played for the championship of the training league.

The Saturday morning of the championship game was a hot, muggy one, even for the first of June. The boys showed up excited to be playing, but not understanding what the true stakes were for this game. Sure, they knew that this game was to determine the winner of the league, but their interest in this game was not close to their interest in the free suicide coke that they received at its conclusion. Our team and Jim Butler's each played well. Still, I was beside myself. I was a good practice coach, but in games I sometimes lost it. I was tough on kids, especially mine, and I let them know when they were not living up to their potentials. All of this was directed at six- and seven-year-old boys.

Where did all of this hostility come from? I know well that it came from my childhood play. I was a miserable failure, and the fact that I was no athlete constantly ate at me. I didn't like myself or my lack of athletic prowess. Too, kids always made fun of me. I was fat, due mostly to the fact that I never met a chicken leg I didn't like. Mother was a wonderful country cook, which meant one staple in her kitchen was a large can of Crisco. My brothers and I ate plenty, and we consumed two gallons of milk every two days. We were active, but a twenty-four hour exercise program wasn't enough to counteract the intake of that many calories.

My dad made my brothers and me sport marine buzz cuts, and that accentuated our large heads that were stuck on top of skinny necks. The two biggest parts of my body were my head and stomach, both of which were strangely placed on stick figure arms and legs. Maybe worst of all were my teeth. They stuck out of my mouth so far that I ground the roof of my mouth with the lower ones. That buck-toothed appearance led to all the kids calling me "Bucky."

Combining all of those physically unattractive characteristics produced a rather unfortunate looking person—me. What's worse is the fact that I knew how others perceived my appearance–unattractive and unathletic. It was a combination that didn't instill confidence. I took those feelings of failure with me into adulthood, and they festered when I returned to the game that had accentuated my feelings of inferiority years earlier.

In spite of me, the team won the championship game. Hallelujah!!! We screamed and carried on as men and little boys do. That evening a party was held at the community pool. We celebrated with hamburgers, hot dogs, and cake. Then the league trophy was presented to our team. Dallas walked up to the front with the other boys to accept the team and individual trophies, but he lacked any excitement about the situation. He accepted the trophy and brought it to me. I gave him a hug and told him I was proud of him. He hung loosely around my legs until I let go. He failed to return the affection. After a season of ball, he was emotionally and physically drained. I had worked him too hard. Baseball had become a job, not a sport that he could enjoy. Dallas was letting me know through the lack of a hug that he was thrilled for baseball to be finished for the year.

What a great dad I was. I managed to exhaust my son. In the process I had also managed to take the joy of the game from him. I stole the championship from Dallas that season, and it was the only one he ever experienced during his years as a team member in a league. More importantly, I began building a wall between us that would reach the heavens in the years to come. My demanding attitude only stiffened Dallas' resolve not to enjoy a minute of the game his dad loved so much. That was the way he would strike back at me for the things I did to him under the mistaken idea that I was helping.

The Third Time Isn't the Charm

Three years of training league ball isn't fair, especially to the adults who coach. But Billy and I once again mapped out our strategy for developing a winning ball club. As in the season before, Billy would choose the players; he still knew them well. My job was to whip them into shape so that they played together smoothly. Some of our team had moved up to another age group, and that meant we'd have a bunch of new kids. Some would be good players, and some would be marginal ones at best.

That third year almost proved to be my undoing. The players that we chose weren't good. Dallas and William stayed with us, but other than them, the team was weak. We had to take a brother-sister pair, but we had to count them as two separate draft selections. No, nothing about training league was close to "real" baseball, and this draft was just another in a long list of examples.

Billy and I saw our fates during the first practice. Kids couldn't stop a ground ball, they couldn't catch a fly ball, and they had no clue how to hit the ball. The sister of the duo we had chosen turned out to be one of the better players on the team. Her brother, however, wasn't so fortunate. He had that dazed look in his eyes, and he hid behind an evil-looking grin. During the entire season the little guy might have come up with one hit. I saw these two children years later as high school students at the school where I taught. The sister grew into a pretty young lady. The brother, still sporting the "deer in the headlights" look and the evil grin, focused his attentions on a different sport—soccer. I was told that he was only slightly better at this sport than he was at baseball.

Another little boy reminded me of Pigpen from the "Charlie Brown" comics. His uniform always was dirty. We didn't know if he played in it at home or if his mom didn't wash the uniform. I suspected the latter was true because the child actually reeked. His parents didn't insist upon cleanliness, and I suspect they had never heard that it was "next to Godliness." His baseball cap brim never was worked so that it curved. Instead, the brim was straight across the front (a look popular today), and when the child put it on his head, he failed to adjust the strap in the back. So, the cap accentuated ears that already stuck out, and the boy's entire appearance had an eerie resemblance to Goober from the old "Andy Griffith" television show of the '50's. In addition, he never wore underwear. On more than one occasion the child told about his lack of them, especially when we asked him to slide. He informed us that he wasn't about to slide on the ground and tear the flesh on his bottom.

The amazing thing about this child was his indifference to the game. He proclaimed himself to be the best of players, when in actuality, his bat rarely made contact with the ball and his glove never caught a ball that wasn't dropped into it by himself or a coach. We placed this boy in right field, the "no man's land" in baseball for the absolute worst players. Doing so had no effect on the boy, mainly because he had no idea what we were doing or why we were doing it. The youngster occupied himself by standing in his position, swaying back and forth, and sticking his middle finger up at the spectators. Several times Billy or I talked to the child, but he ignored us and continued what he realized would drive us to distraction. Neither did his parents correct his behavior. They found his shooting birds hilarious. No, the acorn never falls far from the tree. He never ran after a ball hit in his direction. The boy lazily strode to its location, picked it up, looked at it, and at times made an attempt to throw it. His skills were so poor that the ball might go to the intended player, or it might go flying out of bounds or to the opposite side of the field. At times the boy forgot to release the ball as he hurled it, and it plunked into the ground at his feet.

Another child on the team was a runt. He was no more than half the size of the other players. This boy was at every game, and he brought a cheering section consisting of every member in his extended family. Another disadvantage of this boy was a pair glasses with lenses as thick as the bottoms of old coke bottles. In fact, the child was probably legally blind. He, too, played in the outfield where the chance of his being clobbered by a baseball was minimized. His only hits came when his bat accidentally came in contact with the ball. The poor little guy was so weak and sight impaired that he usually swung after the ball hit the catcher's mitt. Still, he stood at the plate and mouthed his intentions to knock the ball out of the park. He stood there until he hit the ball or one of us coaches told him that he had struck out. In every situation, the little rascal smiled.

The worse we played as a team, the more I harassed Dallas. He was a good player, and if he or William didn't produce hits and runs, as well as cover all ground balls on defense, the team was destined to lose. Both Dallas and I came to dread practices and games. Those evenings ended with a dad who demanded the impossible from his son and with a son who tried to give it. Dallas's third year of ball wasn't filled with charm, and the championship team of which he was a part seemed to have been one from years ago.

My frustrations spurted out in angry attacks. The kids on the team had less fun because I fussed at them. Dallas prayed that he did things correctly so that I didn't embarrass him by stomping to the field and chewing him out in front of the team. I quibbled over the smallest of calls that umpires made because I looked for any possible edge that we could find to help this team have some success. My wife avoided me at all costs after games. She decided asking Dallas about the game was less explosive than talking to me.

During that year Billy and I began a ritual. After each game he came to my house, and we spent hours reliving each play of the ballgame. We sat outside under my carport, a place where we could enjoy our tobacco and throw around profanities. Too, we could sit in the summer night and berate ourselves for coaching mistakes and discuss the kids on the team and how poorly they performed. The irony of the year is that we knew that the team would be horrendous, but we still worked and planned ways to win games. I couldn't let things go, and it was Billy who came to Dallas' rescue when I was about to throw another conniption.

Baseball wasn't about kids and playing anymore. It was about my reputation as a coach. I felt the need to prove to others that I was a good coach, that I could lead a winning team, and that I possessed the knowledge of the game to be a good tactician. Once again, I'd let my inabilities to do things cloud my judgment of how to coach and, more important, how to develop a relationship with my son. All that came from the third year was a wish from everyone that the season would hurry up and mercifully end.

Movin' On Up

The next year Dallas moved to the next level. He now was in Farm League. That name in some way sounded strange for a baseball level. The field dimensions were expanded, and now coaches threw pitches over-handed, the way things are done regularly in baseball. That was about the only thing that mirrored the game. Teams were still drafted, but now coaches stayed in the dugouts. From that vantage point they yelled instructions to their defensive teams. One defensive player still stood in the pitcher's circle, runners couldn't steal bases, and everyone had to bat. The entire two years was too much like another nightmare, and I tried to forget the players and games. Still, some interesting things with players, other coaches, and a father and his son stuck in my mind throughout the years.

Two players made impressions upon me, although they were for opposite reasons. First was the player that everyone in the league had talked about. His size and strength were supposed to guarantee our team's success. The boy proved to be physically strong, although he never hit a home run the entire season. His former coaches had lobbed the ball to him, and while he murdered the baseball then, he never learned how to hit properly. Most of his contacts with the ball were fly outs or weak ground balls. Dallas, half the boy's size, out-hit this strapping youth, yet Dallas wasn't known for his overpowering prowess with the bat.

The other thing about this youngster was his acerbic attitude. Stubborn possibly more accurately described him. He was apt to throw fits when no hits came, and because I was the pitcher, I received the brunt of his ire. To accommodate him, Billy replaced me as the pitcher. The boy stuck out because Billy didn't throw the ball fast enough. The child grew more frustrated, and so did his parents. They began to talk about Billy and me and the horrendous jobs we were doing in coaching their son. Without warning, the boy began to miss games, and by the end of the season, the players and coaches never looked for him. If he did come to a game, he sat the bench until the last innings. I insisted that a child who didn't attend practices and games be held out while others who had been present played first. I made it clear to Billy that I didn't want the kid on any other teams that I coached. In later years, the boy ran into troubles with school officials for a variety of offenses, the end result of his parents' running interference for him throughout life. He eventually disappeared from the community and hasn't been heard from since that time. He didn't play baseball in high school, and a talent-rich individual fell by the wayside.

The second child hated baseball. His reason for being in the league sat in the bleachers. Her curly hair surrounded a drawn, pale face, and only the lenses of her glasses enlarged her beady eyes. This boy's mother insisted that he play ball. The child possessed no skills to make him a ball player and showed no desire to develop any. He didn't swing the bat when his turn at the plate came. He made no attempt to stop a grounder in front of him or to catch a fly ball. All this orange-haired urchin did was smile. He managed this one act easily. No matter how much I fussed at him about playing well, the lean young boy looked at me and simply smiled.

The boy's mother was not nearly so docile. She spewed forth her fury on me about his playing time. The mother asked why her son was always put into the game at the end. I told her that he didn't want to play and that I wasn't going to force him to do so. In fact, I let her know that I was afraid for his safety when he stepped onto the field. I expected at any time for a baseball to bean this child at any moment, and I wondered whether he would still smile if such a thing occurred. The mom didn't like what I said, but she left me alone for the remainder of the season.

The saddest boy on the team was a chunky little guy who grinned and bubbled with excitement. He wanted to play ball and participated in every skill developer that we had. He always came to practice. Sadly, his parents brought him, he hopped out of the vehicle, and the car drove away. When practices were completed, either Billy or I sat with the boy until they returned. The problem became so serious that we called a parent meeting. For the first time that I could recall, Billy showed his anger.

"Some of you parents are bringing your boys to practices and games and then are leaving. According to the rules of the league, someone who is responsible, a parent or guardian, should be at the field throughout the practice or game. Joe and I serve as coaches. We don't serve as babysitters or as shuttle services for your kids."

He concluded with an ultimatum that shocked parents and me.

"The next time you dump one of your sons, he will be dismissed from the team!"

We paid the price for the meeting within a couple of days. The guilty dad showed up at the game, and he proved to be in an especially obnoxious mood. As he swore, he tried to pick a fight. At that younger age neither Billy nor I was afraid to go a couple of rounds with the man, but for the sake of his son, we told him to leave the ballpark. This riled him more as his face reddened and his fists clenched, and at that point, I realized that the man was reeling from too much booze. That infuriated me. I told him to leave right then, and I also had someone to call the police. When the man heard the words "law enforcement," he cut a trail out of the park and squealed the tires of his old beat up car as he pulled onto the highway. The little boy never played another game, and I always felt sorry that he had to put up with such a lousy parent. It was an ironic thought.

The most ridiculous thing about this baseball league concerned umpires, just like years before. On every weeknight but Wednesday, two games were scheduled. The coaches of the two teams that played the second game arrived early to umpire the first game. During the second game, the coaches from the previous one officiated. I attributed such an asinine idea to poor planning, but the fact of the matter was that the people who ran the league were too stingy to pay high school boys to call the games.

The entire concept was filled with potential controversy, and arguments erupted nearly every night. A man would make a call during the first game, and it would incense one of the team's coaches. Right then and there the umpire knew that he had at least one payback call coming during his team's game later in the evening. More than once coaches nearly came to blows, but the league officials stopped the problems with the "You will be thrown out of the league line." If these men who made the threat had spent the money for umpires, no problems would have existed.

I found myself in the middle of several skirmishes with the league officials. Most of them were also coaches in the same league as Billy and me. Practice schedules and game schedules always favored their teams. Rules were enforced against others, but not against them. I challenged the decisions made, and for my efforts I was labeled a troublemaker.

The height of this absurdity was glaringly obvious during a Saturday game. Another coach and I had completed umpiring a game in temperatures that hovered in the low 90s. We dragged our weary, sunburned bodies to the top of the hill where the concession stand stood. We asked for drinks, fountain cokes, and one of the league commissioners handed them to us. Then he said, "That will be seventy-five cents each."

I looked at him incredulously and replied, "You're kidding!"

"NO!" he shot back. "The only ones that get free drinks are the players. Everyone else has to pay."

I argued, "We just finished umpiring a came in this heat, and this league can't spare two fountain drinks?"

As I slid the drink back to the man across the corner, my voice roared, "Keep the damn drink! I wouldn't take anything from this place!"

His comeback was a threat, "You better watch your language around these kids! I'll have you kicked out of this league!"

"Go ahead. See if I give a damn," I spit back.

Over the next year I would run up against other board members. Those men tried every thing possible to oust me from the league. Yet, most of the parents liked me, and Billy was a consummate politician who kept me in the league. Yet, I held such contempt for them that I didn't care if they kicked me out. I would have missed the opportunity to perform all that extra work for free!

During the time in Farm League, Dallas and I began to have deeper problems. No arguments took place, but I increasingly berated him for committing mistakes both in the field and at bat. Dallas was a mule which I worked into a lather on the ball field. In the heat of days he would face the assaults of baseballs whizzing toward him. He stood at the plate as what must have been thousands of baseballs came toward him. He hit some, and some hit him. Rarely did he receive the praise that he deserved. Instead, I analyzed every play that he failed to complete. I lectured him as to what he should have done. His performance as a batter received the same criticism.

How contradictory that sounded. I harangued him because I loved him. I wanted him to taste success. I loved him enough to push him to excel. If he hated me in the process, I allowed it because someday I imagined his telling me how much he appreciated what I had done.

That's why I yelled and screamed at him in the car as we rode home from a game. That's why he and I sat on the front steps and cried when we got home. I cried for having hurt the only son I had, one of persons I most loved in the world. Dallas cried because he thought that he'd failed me. He cried because he was eight and nine years old and didn't understand what I was doing or why I was doing it.

Most of all, I knew that he didn't deserve it.

LAST GO ROUND

The spring that Dallas began playing in the minor league, the next level for boys, two amazing things happened. First, Billy and I did not coach together. At nine my son decided that the time had come for him to play under a different coach. That also meant that I would not be coaching Dallas, another first.

This experiment in changing coaches offered Dallas an opportunity to play ball on his own terms. Billy, who had become my best friend, began to sound just like me in Dallas' ears, and he shut out Billy's help as soon as he began to talk. Being selected to play on a new ball club gave my son the ability to enjoy the game, or so he thought. Billy's feelings were hurt, and I suppose he wanted me to tell Dallas that he had to play for us again. That wasn't going to happened, especially since at home Amy was suggesting strongly that I let Dallas have his way in this situation.

A man named Jack picked Dallas for his team. He knew that Dallas was a good, solid ball player who had become one of the best in the league. He could play the infield. More importantly, the minor league was the first year where boys pitched. Dallas could throw the ball across the plate, and most kids couldn't hit hard enough to get the ball out of the infield. Unlike most other players, Dallas had also progressed to the point that he could reach base most of times that he batted. Jack realized that Dallas could be a huge advantage to him and the team.

The other boys Jack chose weren't that good. He did not know the players in the league well enough to select position players or even individuals who could make the team stronger overall. As a result, many of the players on this team were dumped into his lap, and the overall team lacked skill or athletic ability. The Marlins, the team name for this bunch, were in for a long season, and of course, I lamented over Dallas' being on such a weak team.

One boy who played on the team was the coach's son. This towheaded kid was thin to the point of looking fragile. His greatest weakness, however, became his attitude. Whenever something failed to please him, he pouted to the point of crying. Whether he missed a ground ball, failed to catch a throw to first base, or struck out, this child's eyes filled with tears, and he stomped off, back-talked his dad, and blamed someone else for his misfortune. I watched, amazed, as his dad said nothing to him. Instead, he hugged the boy and patted him and told him things were all right. As I saw it, Jack simply reinforced the boy's inappropriate behavior, but of course, no one asked my opinion.

Another boy on the team could easily have stood in as the first one's twin. This child had the same build and a head of blonde hair. He cared little for the game, another case of a child's playing because a parent insisted. The boy gave little effort, but his smile in some way endeared him to all. That didn't get him a hit or help him stop a ground ball. His parents' coddling only encouraged his behavior problems in later years. The boy became involved with prescription medications during his high school years, and it was rumored that he peddled them to other high school students and abused them himself.

Yes, Dallas told me that he didn't want me to coach him anymore. I knew that my constant carping took an emotional toll on him, and even though I wanted to stay active, I agreed. However, fate denied Dallas' wish. Of the players on the team, only I was a constant father figure who had the slightest idea about coaching. Jack asked me to be his assistant, something that I didn't want to happen, but I knew that he needed the help working with the kids. Jack's background included some time as a baseball player, but being able to play and being able to coach were two entirely different things. Because I was never an athlete but could teach school, I knew the best ways to explain skills to boys who were terrible players with no a speck of ability. In so many ways, I coached my own childhood.

I talked with Dallas about Jack's request, and immediately he reminded me that I had promised not to coach. I explained the dilemma that the team faced with no other man to help Jack. Dallas looked at me disgustedly, and then with resignation in his voice, he groaned "OK." My son was stuck with me for another year, although he didn't want to be.

Actually, Dallas and I handled the year well. I praised him more than usual, and he played well. Of course, with me as his father, many opportunities for my personal actions to completely embarrass the boy presented themselves time and again. The worst of these occurred during a game against an excellent team whom we needed to beat. I was tired of these men always winning and then lording their success over other teams.

At the beginning of the season, the president of the league sent down an edict that all parents would sit in stands located in the outfield. No fan was allowed along the sides of the field. On too many occasions in the past, parents brought lawn chairs and parked themselves behind the backstop or along the base lines. There, some of these people delighted in harassing umpires, high school and college students, and a few times irrational and infuriated parents made threats or actually tried to reach umpires to fight. Other moms and dads amused themselves by heckling the opposing team's players when they batted. Several times I told parents to knock off the behavior, and I was then cursed and jeered. At least the parents left the kids alone. Parents opposed the newly implemented seating arrangement, but as always, few had the courage to stand up to those who made the rules. Instead, they whined at the coaches of the teams and asked them to demand the rule be rescinded, but no coach ever made such a request.

During the night that we played this arrogant team, the president of the league meandered onto the field and took a seat in the dugout. His son was playing first base for that team. Throughout that game this father/league president coached the team, and he made several disparaging remarks about our players. Finally I could take no more, and I stood outside the opponent's dugout and confronted him. For the hundredth time, this league official threatened to throw me out of the league, something of which I wasn't afraid. I told the man,

"You set the rule for parents to sit in the outfield, didn't you?"

His only reply was a weak "Yes,"

"Are you one of the coaches on this team—one that is listed on the roster?"

The man knew where I was headed with this discussion, and he spit out,

"I am the president of this league!"

I pushed him more.

"I don't care if you're president of the U.S.; you aren't one of the coaches though, are you?"

"No," he said reluctantly.

"Then get your ass out of that dugout and go sit where you make the other parents sit!"

The livid man burst from the dugout door and screamed,

"You can't talk like that in front of these kids. You're kicked out of this league forever, starting right now!"

I sneered at him and replied,

"You can't throw me out of this league, and I won't leave. You and your buddies think you can run over everyone else, but I'm not going to let you run over me."

On the way home that night, Dallas emotions wavered. On the one hand, he was proud that his dad stood up to the man. On the other hand, he was tremendously embarrassed by my explosion and subsequent altercation with another parent. I didn't do the right thing either way. My assurance to Dallas that he wouldn't be thrown out of the league provided him with little consolation. Again, his dad ruined what was supposed to be a fun time of playing baseball. By the way, the guy never was able to get rid of me!

In several games Dallas proved to himself that he was a good player. He made his share of spectacular plays at second. He moved to his left well and could go deep into the hole to snare a ball. He also backhanded the ball confidently and then pivoted to make the throw to first. His pitching improved each game. He threw fastballs, but he changed the speeds and located them with pinpoint precision, something special for a boy that young who is in his first year of pitching. He began to see that he was better than the average player—good enough to play on better teams.

Throughout that season, Dallas and I continued to talk about baseball. I remained his stiffest critic, and all too many times I pressed him too hard. Several nights we sat under a clear sky during the late days of spring. We cried again, made promises again, and hung on to each other, but we both knew that our relationship would be a rocky one whenever baseball was involved.

THE BEGINNING OF REAL BASEBALL

After one year of minor league ball and all of the problems with the league board members, I withdrew Dallas from teams and took him to what is called open-league ball. This is where "real" baseball is played. Tryouts are conducted, and only the best players make traveling teams. The risk was enormous, not for me but for Dallas, but this dad decided the time had come for my son to become a baseball player or to leave the sport completely. Of course, I wasn't about to let that happen as long as I could push the boy.

Throughout the winter Dallas and I worked on his game. Countless nights were spent in the high school's back gym. There Dallas scooped up hundreds of ground balls that I hit to him. They weren't easy to capture since the balls took strange hops from the wooden floor and skidded much faster than they did on dirt surfaces. No matter the speed of any ball I hit, Dallas gamely went after it. Sometimes he grew discouraged and smacked his thigh with his glove. I stopped the exercises sometimes to give pointers such as not flipping his glove, keeping his backside down and his knees bent, and watching the ball all the way into his glove. Next, I would have him practice taking a crow hop after he fielded the ball.

After several minutes of fielding, we moved to pitching. At his age, I wouldn't allow Dallas to throw a curveball. I had him work on throwing and controlling his fastball. The speed from it wasn't exceptional; his placement of the ball, however, was excellent. He could pitch the ball low and could work it inside and outside. More than anything, I worked Dallas on his mechanics. Over the years several coaches told me that an average pitcher could become successful if he developed sound mechanics and kept the ball down. So, I subjected Dallas to hours of work in those areas.

Sometimes he grew tired, and his beet-red face showed his exhaustion. I asked him if he wanted to quit, but his answer was always "no." He knew that is what I expected of him, and he didn't want to disappoint me. I was aware that he needed a break, but a dad too wrapped up in his son's success loses what good judgment he has. Dallas threw approximately fifty pitches at each session.

Our next activity was long throw. We stood facing each other, and as we threw the ball, we separated ourselves until we stood at opposite ends of the gym. This exercise strengthened his arm, not only for pitching but also for throwing to first base. Dallas enjoyed this drill because during it we relaxed, threw the ball, and talked as dads and sons should talk.

The last station in our routine was the one that Dallas hated: hitting. I threw the ball to him in a batter's cage in the upper deck of the gym. Like other times, I threw the ball harder than most dads. I wanted Dallas to be able to hit any pitches that might zip toward him. On several occasions, I hit him, and I knew that the contact hurt. Even though I felt miserable for having popped him, he stood in for the next pitch, and he glared at the ball and me with tears welling up in his eyes.

I became ferocious during these hitting sessions. My tirades covered Dallas' failure to watch the ball, swing through the ball, step to the ball, etc. I gave the kid so many different orders that he couldn't remember what to do. He was anxious and tentative so as to not make a mistake, but I groused at him for those very things. He swung at between one and two hundred pitches each session, enough so that his hands blistered. More than anything, Dallas wanted to hit the ball hard and straight—straight toward my head. I know that he would have found those nights of torture worthwhile if he could have one time hit a ball that flattened my nose or blacked one of my eyes.

As we continued the gym workouts, I critiqued him on his performance and lectured him on what skills he needed to improve. Then we went to a convenience store where I bought him a drink. At home, he pretended to finish any homework and then played video games until bedtime. During the rest of the night he usually had no contact with me, but when we did speak, his answers to any questions I might have had were curt.

In early spring I began scouring the sports pages in the local paper for teams who were looking for players. One was holding tryouts at a ballpark close to our house, so I informed Dallas that we would be attending them on the date given. No, I never gave my son the chance to decide about whether he wanted to participate.

On that Saturday morning we left the house for the ball field. The air was still cold, and a frost covered the grass. Dallas wore sweat pants and top, along with thick socks and cleats. I talked to him during the short ride and told him not to be nervous, as if that were possible. I, on the other hand, was crazy with anxiety. He had the skills to make the team; all he needed to do was put them into action. I needed only to have a little faith in my son.

Upon arrival Dallas saw a swarm of boys, and as always, he withdrew. His shyness always kept him from making friends easily. We found the coach, Brian Ownby, and I introduced Dallas. The coach turned his attention toward my son, and his encouraging voice immediately resonated in Dallas' heart. Brian told him to join the other boys, and with that I was dismissed to the stands where I nervously watched every move that Dallas made.

During that tryout, I don't remember Dallas missing a single ball. He performed wonderfully, and my chest stuck out like that of a rooster leading his harem into the yard. Dallas' skills in the outfield weren't nearly as good, and he ran down few of the balls hit to him. His batting was good, but nothing that would turn heads. Brian, however, told the boys that he was looking at their swing and didn't care if they hit a single ball.

Other boys at the tryout were equally good ball players. Brian Sprowl and Derrick Milligan were two that showed exceptional skills. Brian was a shortstop, and I knew immediately that Dallas would be moved to a new position if he made this team. All in all, Coach Ownby had put together a solid group of boys. He told them and parents that they would receive a phone call in the evening if they were to return to the second day of tryouts.

I panicked! "What's this about a second day of tryouts? When in the evening will the phone call come? When will the final decision be made as to who makes the team?"

Dallas was less than concerned. The day's activities had sapped his energy, and after a bath he lumbered toward bed for a long nap. He had performed the best that he could and had no intentions of worrying about the outcome. I envied him for his cool manner and calm approach because the rest of the afternoon and evening tortured me unmercifully until Brian called.

The second day of tryouts turned out to be a means of spotting boys in the positions that they would play during the season. As I had predicted, Dallas' new home on the diamond was second base. He shared time there with another boy, one who wasn't half as skilled as Dallas and played no more baseball after that season. Coach Ownby put the boys through the drills. They worked on fielding and throwing; some boys, including Dallas, spent time on the pitching mound as they worked on delivering pitches to home and holding runners at first base. Hitting practice took quite some time, and then Brian coached them about stealing bases and stretching leads. Finally, he ran the boys. I knew Dallas was miserable then. Like his dad, Dallas hated to run. To do it in a game where the action came naturally wasn't a big deal. However, Dallas viewed sprints for conditioning as nothing more than cruelty by any coach who might employ them.

Little by little, Brian Ownby molded the boys into a solid team, one that could compete with almost every other one in Knoxville. The two that became our nemeses were the Knoxville Stars and The Thunder. These teams came from baseball schools where boys were hand-selected from as far away as one hundred miles. Still, the Junior Vols proved to be a strong team with plenty of ability.

The thought never occurred to me to ask Dallas if he was happy about being on the team. I assumed that he shared my excitement. He was happy that I was pleased about his making the team, but Dallas was unable to decide whether making a traveling team was something that he wanted. He told me that he was afraid it would take too much time. When I asked him "from what?" he told me to forget it.

The team played in a league, as well as in weekend tournaments. The first weekend tournament was played in frigid weather. Our car was filled with the family, and each of us paid $5 to watch Dallas play, a hefty price during those times. Most fans complained about the charges, but the park people hosting the event told us they needed to make enough money to pave the parking lot. The concession stand prices were exorbitant, and by the end of the weekend tournament, I was considering borrowing money to pay for this new type of baseball life.

Dallas' team won its first game played at 8 p.m., and the boys faced a team from Kingsport the next day. This team, like the two in Knoxville, was an elite one, and the boys had played together since their first year of organized ball. Too, they dwarfed our boys. The team lost the game and a great deal of their confidence. The tournament ended on Sunday as parents and players huddled under a picnic shed and waited for the rain to end. It never did, so we called it a day and went home. I learned that traveling teams didn't necessarily play all the games scheduled and that the key word for survival was "adapting," something I'd never learned to do.

One tournament took us to Greenville, Tennessee, and another took us to Kingsport. We played poorly in the first, but we competed intensely in the second one. In fact, an earlier loss to the Kingsport team was avenged. However, the game against the Knoxville Thunder was a nightmare. Most of their players were a year older than ours, and they were, in fact, a better team. What caused pain was the way that team beat our boys. The coach had no desire to show any mercy or sportsmanship. His team was in complete control and the outcome had long ago been decided, but he continued to steal bases, bunt, and run the score up. The boys on that team stood in the dugout and made fun of our players. In the end The Thunder won the ballgame, but they lost the respect of some of their own fans. Of course, their coach was in no way affected; he continued to demand his "machine" play ball and humiliate other teams.

The Junior Vols won their own tournament that year. Each boy received a medallion strung to a ribbon of red, white, and blue. Dallas took his home, placed it on a shelf above his bed, and never touched it again. He played in most games during the season, but no sign of positive emotions shown through. He did his job on the field, and when the game ended, he put it out of his minded, or at least pretended to. No boy ever seemed to care less about baseball.

Probably his most memorable moments of the season came in two different tournaments. The first was a local tournament at Inskip. Dallas was the designated pitcher for this game. I don't recall the opponent, but I do remember that through four innings, Dallas had pitched a no-hitter. Inexplicably, Brian replaced him with another boy in the top of the fifth and last inning. The other boy managed to save the no-hitter, but no one ever understood why Coach Ownby made the move. Dallas on that day showed emotions. He was furious because he knew that he was close to finishing the no-hitter that he had started. The other special moments occurred at another local tournament at Badgett Field. On Sunday the team had reached its last game. Brian decided to mix things up. Dallas was granted his wish to play catcher. It's questionable whether or not the boy stopped a single pitch. He allowed base runners to advance as if they were riding a merry-go-round. However, that day Dallas enjoyed playing baseball as he never had before. It was one of the few times I saw him excited on a ball field, and to this day, he still remembers the game he played catcher.

Throughout the season, Dallas contended with two problems. One was the other boy who played second base. Dallas wanted to play, but he understood the sharing of time. His other problem was bigger and more imposing: his dad. I constantly yelled out to Dallas during games and gave him helpful hints. My incessant yelling at and to him distracted him from the game. Between innings I would walk to the dugout and call Dallas to the side. Then I would give him a mini-course in hitting or fielding or I would harass him for his poor play.

Again, the vicious routine began. The rides after games included lectures and excoriations. Arrival at home led to time on the front steps and tears. It was a cycle to which I subjected my son but had no idea of how to end. Dallas grew more and more frustrated with what he perceived to be his inability to play to the level that I deemed good. I tormented him, and yes, I unintentionally abused him.

BASEBALL SCHOOLS

Dads are the reason for baseball school, also known as baseball academies. They've popped up throughout the Southeast in the last few years with no lack of clientele. Some of these businesses also have served a major role in destroying the game of baseball.

The most popular academy in the South is probably the East Cobb Baseball organization. This school offers its own complex with fields and training facilities. Staff members include former big leaguers, and kids flock to them for lessons in hitting and catching. The organization might list itself as a nonprofit, but instructors don't give instruction for nothing. Teams affiliated with this organization also participate in fundraisers by selling ads in the media guides and sponsorships. Its website lists fifty-six teams for players ages eight through eighteen. Locally, teams with academies have stationed themselves at stoplights and panhandled from waiting cars.

Baseball schools charge fees that sometimes place hardships on families. It's not unusual to charge a player several hundreds or thousands of dollars for the season. Additionally, travel expenses are enormous as these elite teams travel throughout the southeastern United States. Of course, some players are automatically excluded because of the financial burdens. Men with ties to the organization usually are the coaches of these teams. During the off-season, team members are required to practice at the schools, and they are charged a monthly fee. It's not unusual for a team with twelve players to pay $600 a month or more for this practice time. All of these expenditures are in addition to the costs of cleats, gloves, and bats, which together can add another $500- $1000 to the costs. What's more, shoes and bats don't last more than one year.

Baseball schools that existed when Dallas played ball were strong organizations. The Knoxville Stars was the oldest group. Later the Dodgers organization appeared, as did the Knoxville Thunder. Then, The Yard and The Impact became the big names. The last three became academies. Only the Stars began with the idea of bringing Knoxville athletes the opportunity to play quality baseball, but even that group fell victim to the bad parts of open league ball.

Baseball schools are notorious for siphoning the best talent from all leagues in their areas. In the end, the community ball leagues are filled with weak players who can't possibly compete with them. Many of these teams withdraw from local recreation leagues and play only in weekend tournaments. Sometimes schools go outside the area to recruit a boy. I recall one player for an academy who drove over one hundred miles for practices. He took a position that could have been offered to a local player.

Baseball schools are businesses. Investors look for returns on their moneys, and coaches are well aware of it. Those coaches face much the same pressures that college and professional coaches face: win or lose your team. But winning is only part of the demand. Academy teams need to win big if they plan to keep a steady flow of players coming through the doors. In too many games coaches of theses teams keep the starters in and continue to play aggressively, even though the outcome has been decided. In the process of showing the dominance of the organization, elite teams humiliate other ones.

Elitist attitudes led to other things. Boys who made these teams began to believe that they were better than the rest of the kids with whom they went to school. Their feelings of superiority carried over in the classroom. Academy ballplayers belittled those whom they defeated. During ball games these boys displayed a complete lack of sportsmanship. They laughed at mistakes by other players and harassed them throughout the game. Many times they refused to shake hands at the end of games due to that lack of sportsmanship. No one could lay the complete blame on the boys. They were the products of their coaches. The men in charge of them had taught them to be insensitive to other players; they taught those kids to win at all cost.

The brand of ball that academies teach isn't at all what boys of earlier generations played. Today's kids are expected to play year-round. By fall academy teams have been chosen, and they participate in fall leagues and showcases. There, scouts for colleges and even professional ball evaluate kids and their playing ability. Winter months are spent at the schools where teams practice a couple of times each week. Additionally, individual boys take lessons and work with weight or personal trainers. By February teams are outside taking fielding practice. Teenaged players begin their school seasons where they can play thirty or more games. Then summer ball begins. Teams with players as young as eight can play a sixty-game schedule. By the time school begins, these boys are exhausted, but the year begins again. This type of schedule continues until the teen graduates and begins his career as a college or professional player. Baseball becomes a job, not a game that kids enjoy. Sure, they might like the scholarships that they earn or the minor league contracts that they sign, but too many of them burn out. The game stopped being fun years earlier, and by the time high school is over, many athletes hang up their spikes, gloves, and bats for good.

The first sentence I wrote stated that Dads are the reason for baseball schools. I was one of them. I looked at my son and had visions of grandeur. I taught him all that I could, but his skills still weren't what I considered good enough. I contacted coaches who were friends, and they gave Dallas lessons. My friend Billy began a school in a neighboring town, and Dallas spent time there. More hitting lessons and pitching lessons came on evenings when he was tired or when he would have preferred playing a video game. I wouldn't hear of it. Dallas needed work, and I knew what was best for him.

Other dads are just as bad. We want the glory of our sons' accomplishments. We spend the family fortune on promises made by baseball school owners. Seeing our sons in those elite uniforms swells our pride.

Funny thing is Dallas never played on a single one of those academy teams. No matter how much I denied it, he wasn't a good enough ball player to make those teams. Sure, he was a solid, above-average athlete, but he couldn't compete consistently with kids more physically gifted. The fact was my son never wanted to compete with or against those academy players. He wanted to play a game that he enjoyed, but he didn't want it to become his entire life.

Plenty of folks have claimed my dislike for baseball schools is sour grapes because Dallas didn't make any team. Probably there's some truth in that. More than that is my twenty-twenty hindsight. I see what baseball became because of overbearing dads who pushed their sons over the limit and the businessmen who took advantage of our flaws. Each dad that loaded up his son in the car and drove him to a lesson where he swung a bat until his hands blistered or pitched until his arm ached all the way to the bone kept those schools in business. Every dad might well have turned his son against baseball just as I did with my son. I hope today's dads are smarter than I was.

A Year in Baseball Hell

The worst year of baseball started out as the best one. Billy decided that he wanted to put a team together that could compete with the baseball academies in the area. Billy was a pure recruiter. In fact, I am confident that he could help any college team with its needs. His uncanny ability to help players visualize their talents and how they fit a team earned him the utmost respect.

So, he set out to put his plan into action. The name of the team was the Smokies. By the time Billy had finished his pursuit of players, we had a team to be reckoned with. Of course, two of the boys to play on the team were William and Dallas, and each boy legitimately belonged on it.

Billy entered the team into a fall league to keep the players sharp, but some played basketball and could not join until the spring. He quickly phoned other boys, and in no time the fall league team was set. He and I would coach them. Things worked well, and we began the season winning our games. Only one team gave us trouble; it was comprised of players from one of the baseball schools, and the coaches were two men who were more unpleasant than I was.

I never was a success in sports. As an elementary school student, I was fat and slow, but I made up for those two things with my incredible weakness. In short, no one ever mistook me for an athlete. In basketball, I couldn't shoot, but I could pass to the open men who could make the shots. In baseball, I couldn't hit nor could I catch nor could I stop a groundball too well. In football, I blocked well enough to keep my man from making all of the tackles.

High school athletics was no kinder to me. I played freshman football, and I actually started at left guard and middle linebacker. My twin brother Jim played too, and I was given credit for anything positive that either of us accomplished. During the second year, headaches became so debilitating that I quit the team. Then I became its manager, the guy who passed out uniforms and pads and washed dirty clothes and towels. In fact, that first year as a manager, I was the only person connected with the team to sustain a season-ending injury. I broke my ankle carrying dry footballs on the field during one soggy Friday night.

I knew what the kids at school thought of me. "Jock washer" wasn't an affectionate name that players gave me. The frustration of being athletically challenged and publicly ridiculed caused more and more anger to bubble just under the skin. A fight here or there might have eased the pain, but I avoided them as much as possible. Jim, my brother, was the fighter, and his reputation kept others from attacking me.

Even in college, I managed to sprain both ankles at the same time in one intramural football game, and in softball, a pitch with no arc zinged off the bat and straight back into my stomach; it knocked me off my feet and left an ugly bruise the perfect shape of the ball. In my last hurrah as a ball player, I was known in the church league as the only man ever to have hit a home run but ended up as a triple because I was so slow.

Dallas' misfortune was to be my son, and he suffered the rigors of training in the sport that I chose for him. He inherited the same slowness of foot.

His disposition was much different, more like his mother's than mine. I would scream and fuss and demand. Dallas swallowed all those negative emotions. Eventually, that suppression would cause irritable bowel syndrome and bouts of depression. He spent much of his time in a hell that I made for him.

The night of the fall league championship game arrived, and we played our nemesis again. Throughout the game each team played with determination and genuine dislike for the opposing side. During one of our turns at bat toward the end of the game, Billy questioned a call. I stood in the first base coach's box, right outside the opponent's dugout and across the chain link fence from their fans. The two coaches yelled at my partner to shut up. I, in turn, turned and told them,

"Sit your asses down and shut your mouths."

At the same time one of the other team's fans yelled at me, and I kissed my hand and then patted my butt with it. Immediately, the umpire threw me out of the game. As I was walking out, the head coach snorted some comment, and again I told him to sit his ass down. He charged me, and we squared off right in front of the dugout. Umpires and other coaches stepped between us.

All the while, Dallas watched this scene in disbelief. He defended his dad at first, but then he stopped because in his heart he realized that I deserved every punishment that could be handed out. Immature actions of his dad embarrassed him. On the way home I fumed about the injustice of the affair, but Dallas remained silent. Arriving at home, he left the car, went to his room, and shut the door. I was left to explain the story to his mother, and she instantly grew furious with me.

The season ended with a dark pall hanging over our household. Others might have enjoyed my ridiculous actions, but my son and wife were simply embarrassed by them. Throughout the winter months I took Dallas to the high school again to work on every phase of the game. He continued to play second base, just as his cousin had done, and his reflexes continued to be quick and his hands remained soft; I decided that he needed to constantly work to refine his abilities during the off-season.

The boy ran stiff, as stiff as a dead man. His every movement, from picking up his feet to pumping his arms, looked mechanical. Dallas always cast an image of a boy in agony as he ran, and because he was so tense, his stride was all of six inches. His feet flew, but he covered no ground. Others offered to work with him on technique. Dallas even considered working with a former Olympic runner with whom my wife worked, but in the end, he declined. If he didn't run fast, it was no big deal to him. In reality, Dallas knew that I had accepted his slowness, and that was one less thing about which I could harangue him.

The spring began with a new coach for the team that Billy had put together in the fall. Jim, my twin brother, had coached several of his son's teams in years past, and once again Billy turned on the charm until Jim agreed to become the head coach. Our team was a couple of players short of the twelve that we wanted, so we held tryouts. One boy came from Loudon, and he sometimes could pitch well. At other times he was uncontrollable and inconsolable. When he didn't play every game, the child whined and cried to his dad, and the man grew more furious as the season passed. The second boy we chose had only the briefest of tryouts. He was a bit chubby, but he seemed to be suitable for the team. He could hit well, and his fielding was above average. This child's major drawback was his dad. A former college athlete who tried to relive life through his son's time, he proved to be my damnation. I so easily saw this man's weaknesses, but never recognized the same damning qualities in myself.

Practices were surprises to the players. Ever the disciplinarian, Jim used each minute of time drilling players in every phase of the game. He could be encouraging when a boy did well, but his words could also cut to the quick when a boy gave less than his best efforts. Dallas was at the end of many of those tongue-lashings. The other players needed to see that Jim would bawl out his own family and that he would treat everyone the same. Yes, the boys played with a degree of fear of Jim. Yet, they respected him as a coach and realized that he had the abilities to lead the team to its best efforts. Dallas, however, continued to live a miserable existence since now the attacks came from his dad and his uncle. He could find no place to escape.

Jim won the hearts of the players after one particular day of practice. Billy found a ball field in terrible condition. He talked to and made a deal with the commissioner who oversaw it. Billy and I had worked on a field to improve it enough to be a practice field, and we finished with blisters on our hands and aches in our backs. For that work our team was allowed use of the field each week to practice at a specified time. One day we arrived at the field to find a rival team from a baseball school practicing. We thought little of it and waited until our appointed time. However, the other team wasn't stopping its practice; they had ignored us. Jim called out in his friendly voice to the coach,

"Coach, we have the field scheduled for 5:00. We'd appreciate it if you'd wrap things up."

The man looked at Jim and nodded, but he said not a word. We waited another five minutes, and the team worked as if they were in mid-practice. By now, Jim was annoyed, and he walked out on the field.

"Coach, we have the field reserved for now. Get your guys off!"

One of the other coaches stormed toward Jim, and I hurried out to stand with him.

"You can't tell us what to do. We'll use the field as long as we want!"

Jim glared at the man as he bellowed,

"You better get you team off the field, NOW!

By then the head coach reached Jim.

"Who do you think you are?" This field belongs to nobody, and it's first come, first serve."

Jim spun on his heels, burned holes through the man's skull with his stare, gritted his teeth and hatefully said,

"I'm the man who's going to kick your ass if you don't get off this field right now! Joe and Billy worked on this place to get it fit to use, and Billy has the name of the woman who gave us this time if you want to call her!"

With that Jim stood ready for warfare, if that was what the man wanted. Instead, the coach told his boys to get their equipment and get off the field.

That night Jim gave that group of boys more confidence than they had ever had. Most of the team had never beaten a Thunder team on the field of play, but on that one night, the head coach blinked, he gave in, and he left with defeat in his craw.

As play began that year, the boys worked together as a unit. Jim had them performing the fundamentals of baseball, and the knowledge of them helped to make the team successful. Still, a baseball team has nine positions, and twelve names completed our roster. That meant that three boys wouldn't start the game. They probably would see playing time, but they just wouldn't be in the line-up as the game began. Dads didn't like the fact that their sons weren't starting, and before half the season was close to being complete, those dads stood on the hillside during games and bad-mouthed Jim and me constantly. One night, Jim had listened to enough whining from dads, and he quit. Most of the boys, the ones who cared about the team, didn't want him to quit, but three or four dads and their sons had riled Jim to the point that he wasn't going to take any more guff. He didn't have any personal investment in the team and was doing it as a favor to Billy and me. The last thing Jim wanted was to listen to dads whine and then have to prepare to fight them.

Dallas was furious. He had waited for years to play for Jim, and he excelled under Jim's coaching, even though he dreaded the hateful talk from his uncle. Now, the team was stuck with Billy and me again, and although we were successful coaches, we lacked the stature of a coach like Jim. Again, Dallas played ball under conditions for which he was not prepared and about which he was disgusted, but I had no answers to help the situation.

The same dads continued their carping, only this time the barbs were aimed at me. I didn't want to put Dallas in the middle of the mess, so I quit coaching not much later. Sometimes I amazed myself with my naiveties. The moment I stepped aside, the dad whose griping was the loudest filled the void. He was none other than the father of the boy we picked as a member at the last moment, the college athlete who wanted to play again.

John's first move was to bench Dallas. He replaced him with kids who couldn't play the position. However, this man was vindictive, and he knew that the best way to upset me was to unfairly treat my son. He was right.

After watching his cruel behavior for a while, I exploded at one tournament. The team had just lost to a team that had far less talent than the Smokies. However, the kids had been through so much that their hearts were no longer in the game. As usual, Dallas had seen no playing time. I approached John, and I yelled,

"You're an asshole. Only an asshole would use a kid as a way of spiting his dad. You aren't fair, and it's going to stop!"

John stood stunned for a moment, and then he countered,

"You little son-of-a-bitch! I'll whip your ass!"

And with that the melee was on. John outweighed me by seventy-five pounds, and he was taller than I. At that point, I didn't care. I had tears in my eyes, and when I was mad enough to cry, I didn't care what happened, nor did I care what I did. Billy separated us and told me to leave the park. That afternoon the team played the Thunder, but Dallas never stepped on the field except in the closing innings as a pinch hitter.

The next day was Sunday, and Dallas and I arrived at the ballpark early, just as we always did. John arrived, and he came to me and told me that Dallas was off the team. I was incredulous. Here was a team that Billy, Jim, and I had put together and practiced, and now this goon whose son was an afterthought on the team was throwing Dallas off. What amazed me even more was the fact that not one damn parent spoke up on behalf of Dallas, not the catcher's mother, whom I had dealt with when everyone else avoided her, and not Billy, the person whom I had called my best friend. The only thing left to say was that I wanted a full refund on all the money that I had paid for Dallas to be a part of the team. With those closing remarks, I walked my twelve-year-old son to the car. We drove away with our heads held high, but both of us cried the whole way home. I cried for Dallas' lost season and my lost best friend. Dallas cried because he had to live with a maniacal father who had managed to have him kicked off a team that his own dad had helped to form. He also cried because he didn't know if I would ever be smart enough to figure out the problem. The season was half finished, but Dallas had no team on which to play for the rest of the summer. He didn't pick up a glove, ball, or bat, and for once, I didn't demand that he do so. I was too sick over the things that had transpired, and I couldn't understand why Billy hadn't stood with me. Later he told me that his name was on all the bills for the team, and if it folded, he would have to pay the balance of the large debt that had been incurred. The only selfish satisfaction I gained came as I heard stories about the ways that the team fell apart under John's coaching and how he and another dad (Billy had withdrawn from his coaching spot) found incredible ways to lose ballgames. In the end, the boys on the Smokies team experienced a miserable year. I sinned greatly as a father that summer, and I spent my time in hell for it. Hell is more miserable than I imagined.

WHOSE FAULT IS IT?

So, whose fault is it? An apparent epidemic of violence is exploding on playing fields of all kind. The National Association of Sports Officials receives more than one hundred reports a year of physical contact between coaches, players, fans, and officials. At a basketball game a man body slammed a referee for throwing out his wife when she continually yelled obscenities during a game. At a soccer game a player punched the ref after he red-carded the kid for cursing and later taunting.

For me, the bad behavior occurred at baseball games, just like it does for so many others. Plenty of examples were posted on the N.A.S.O. website:

- New Jersey—One parent punched out an umpire at a Babe Ruth league game. A Brownie troop leader stormed the field of a minor league game to protest a call. When she failed to leave, officers handcuffed her and escorted her from the stadium.

- Florida—A coach threw a sucker punch when an umpire turned his back to leave a squabble.
- California—A man knocked an umpire unconscious over a disputed call at a nine- and ten-year-olds league game.
- Louisiana—A father attacked an official in a bathroom and threatened to kill him after the ump ejected both coaches of the assailant's son's team.
- Tennessee—An irate coach approached an umpire and his seventeen-year-old son, who also served as an official. He clobbered the father who had questioned the safety of bats. The ump's son had questioned the same bats the previous night.

The number of incidents increases each year and shows no signs of ebbing. In a survey conducted by *Sports Illustrated for Kids,* a staggering seventy-four percent of the three thousand kids responding said they had seen out-of-control parents at their games. They observed parents who yelled at children, coaches, and officials, as well as coaches who yelled at kids and officials. Four percent stated they had witnessed violent acts by adults. Yes, that number seems small, but one hundred twenty cases is shocking. If it is logical to assume this same percentage holds true for all of baseball (8.6 million players), then at least 344,000 children have witnessed these violent acts at games. We are a nation of adults out of control. I was one of them.

Children mimic our actions, and they become those angry players who fly into rages when things don't go as they expect. "Hey, mom and dad act like fools, and they seem to think it's all right to attack any person who rules against them, so why shouldn't I do the same?" I don't have an answer for any kid that asks that. I am lucky that Dallas' personality is more like his mother's. The thought of becoming physically violent never occurred to him. In too many situations my son spent his time trying to calm down an out-of-control father who was ready to go after any number of officials and other coaches.

Coaches—that's another group that can share the blame for violence. Too many men have the win-at-all-costs mentality. The game itself and the skills and lessons involved are not important. To them, the victory is the sole prize, and they expect players to sell their souls, if need be, in order to come out victorious. Another study conducted by three well-known universities found that thirteen percent of the players surveyed admitted they tried to hurt an opponent, and over one-fourth admitted to being bad sports. Coaches many times push athletes to an appalling level of action. Kids know that some coaches reward aggressive behaviors like these with playing time while boys who play within the rules and spirit of the game tend to see more pine-time.

Plenty of blame is left to pass around, and a big chunk of it can be placed squarely on the shoulders of professional athletes. Kevin Brown was in a bad mood and assaulted a cameraman. Roger Clemens and Mike Piazza exchanged glances, curses, and blows in front of a national audience. Over and over again, managers and players have gone after umpires with whom they disagree on some call. Most of the time the officials are correct in the call, but kids are more interested in the fight than the replay. Our role models have said they don't want that job, but they accept it when the big checks are written to them. They owe the kids who love baseball more than temper tantrums.

Society at large also must accept its share of responsibility for the violent acts of kids and parents. For too many years individuals haven't been held accountable for their actions. It seems as if something else is always the culprit for bad behavior. Maybe a newly discovered physical illness is to blame. Sometimes acting out is declared the result of something like ADHD. We're told that the individual didn't realize what he was doing or couldn't control himself so that he acted in an appropriate manner. Other times, psychological factors are said to be the reason for misbehavior. So many times we're told that an individual's troubled childhood is solely responsible for his actions as an adult. I wonder if all of us at some point have to get over the bad things of the past in order to move on.

Finally, we often hear that violent video games, television shows, and movies teach that violence is an acceptable means of expressing oneself. Any person with an ounce of common sense sees through this feeble excuse. The on-off switches usually work on all those media-playing devices. It's the parents who fail to pull the plug on games that they deem inappropriate.

Sometimes we have to admit the truth. I wish I had seen mine much earlier. Regardless, here it is. I was an over-reacting parent and coach. I placed too much importance upon the game. I treated my son too harshly too often, and I tried to turn a game into a test of manhood. Instead, it glaringly showed the lack of mine. I was wrong so many times, and for that I am ashamed. Above all else, I've apologized to Dallas and to those whom I offended. Yeah, I know it's too little too late, but it's the best I can do now. I'm the parent and coach who is to blame for much of what was wrong with my son's experiences in baseball.

Raw Talent

By the time the spring of 1997 rolled around, Dallas was so nearly disconsolate about baseball that I wasn't sure he would play any more. One thing that was certain was that the year would be more enjoyable than the nightmare he faced the previous summer.

Billy and I had hashed out our differences. I told him how hurt and disappointed he had made me feel by not standing up for my son, someone he had always claimed to be his second son. Through a series of heated exchanges Billy again explained that he was afraid financially during the summer from hell. He had put his name on the bills for all the equipment, uniforms, and tournament fees that the team had incurred. Billy felt sure that the men who had overtaken the team would ignore the bills, coach the remainder of the season, and leave him holding the ticket in the end. As much as I wanted to still be mad at Billy, I couldn't be because I understood the predicament he was in.

As it turned out, Billy had harbored some ill feelings for me for a couple of years. He was furious when Dallas went to his first open-league tryout without inviting William. At that one time, I was being selfish; I wanted Dallas to cut ties with everything in the little league program so that he could prove to himself that he was good enough to play in a better league. I didn't invite William, and Billy's feelings were hurt. I don't blame him.

We held tryouts, and some of the players looked talented during that time. However, as we held practice, their weaknesses became more apparent. In fact, some of these guys performed as if they had never played before. They knew nothing about taking leads, if they ever could somehow manage to reach first base. Some of the boys caught fly balls with fear and uncertainty showing in their body language and radiating from their eyes. On more than one occasion one of these outfielders would run up on the ball and then watch as it sailed over their heads.

One particular boy was a big, strong kid. He could throw the ball as hard as any player that we faced. However, its path was a different matter. Rusty threw the ball and struck out several opponents who swung, not because the pitches were in the strike zone nor because they had fooled them. No, they swung at the ball in self-defense. Boys would walk to the plate with trembling lips and weak knees as they awaited a pitch that just might nail them in the back or in the head. Neither was he a consistent hitter, but Rusty put the bat on the ball just often enough to make him appear to be a scoring threat to other teams.

Stephen was another unusual player. Billy had coached him at the minor league level of little league, and he swore that the kid would help us tremendously. Yet, Stephen never developed his skills past the level at which Billy coached him in earlier years. The boy was left-handed, and he had a vicious curve ball, but for some reason Stephen never wanted to throw the pitch. He only went through the motions of the game and never said more than a couple of words to his teammates or coaches. He also played some first base, but even there he gave minimal effort.

The most interesting character was Joey. The boy couldn't play a lick of baseball. We put him in the outfield, when he played any defense, for one main reason: to prevent his being injured or killed. Joey couldn't catch, couldn't throw, and couldn't bat. His scattered hits came after his head had already pulled around and the ball accidentally hit the bat. If, however, he made contact with the ball, no one threw him out at first because the boy possessed blazing speed. Toward the end of the season, Joey became our designated runner for the pitcher or catcher. On the base, he smiled at everyone, and then he took his lead. No pick-off move to first ever bothered Joey. He didn't know what the pitcher was doing. Joey only cared about running to the next base, and he most often stole second with ease.

During this season Billy and I did our best coaching job ever. We had little talent, so we had to teach fundamentals. Our first scrimmages were brutal affairs with teams beating us by lopsided scores, but as the season progressed, we began to improve to the point that we beat some teams in some tournaments that were far superior to us. Watching a bunch of cocky kids deflate when this rag-tag bunch whipped them was always a satisfying feeling.

The early season Loudon tournament was one that nearly did me in. Our first game was held at about 9 p.m. on a Friday night. The wind felt as if it were gale force, and the temperatures were brutally cold. The Cobras, our team's name, played a team that was better than we were, but the boys went out and played with dogged determination. They were rewarded with a win, something made sweeter because the elements were so extremely unfriendly. The bad news was that we were scheduled to play the next morning in the first game.

That next day brought conditions that were worse than the night before. The wind had picked up considerably, and the skies began to spit snow as the game continued. I had suffered in the cold enough the previous night to cause me to make changes in my wardrobe for the following day. I stood in the first base coach's box. A pair of jeans covered long underwear, and two long-sleeved tops covered thermal underwear. Over these items I wore an insulated zip-up set of coveralls. Thick, insulated gloves covered my hands, and on my head, I wore a cap like the one Ralphie wore in "The Christmas Story." Yes, the bill of the cap flipped up, and the sides of the hat covered ears and jaws and joined under the chin. I wore two pairs of thermal socks and covered them with insulated boots. Most every parent and player with the Cobras laughed at me when I entered the park. Dallas was simply embarrassed—again— about my appearance. By the second inning, those same people began asking me to share some of my cloth-ing with them, but then my turn came for laughter as I teased them about being cold. That day I was the only warm person at the ballpark, and Dallas realized just a little that I wasn't the raving fool that he believed me to be.

We joined a league in Oak Ridge that summer. Granted, the league didn't include the toughest teams in the area, but we didn't want to play that kind of ball during this season. Still, teams were competitive. One Oak Ridge team in particular was out for blood. They played games against us as if the World

Series were at stake. In the end, they wound up tied with us in the league. Not too bad for a bunch of scrub ballplayers.

That year in baseball Dallas moved to another position. His lack of speed had caught up with him. Billy and I talked about this move, and we decided that Dallas' best chance of making a high school team and having the chance to play after that rested on his playing first base. He liked the position, although learning how to use a first baseman's mitt took some time. Dallas possessed the quickness and soft hands to field the ball consistently.

I began to back off Dallas that year. After the preceding year's fiasco, he desperately needed to have some fun in the game. I made an effort to be positive with him as much as was humanly possible for me. He played a bit more laid-back, and the result was that he fielded better, hit tremendously, and pitched with exceptional control. This was his best year yet as a ball player with a dad for a coach. He didn't dread the games that year because no one applied pressure. No one expected the team to be successful, so each boy relaxed and concentrated on improving his skills.

One night in the league, we played the second-scheduled game, the one under the lights. However, the lights went out in the middle of it due to a power failure that blanketed the city in darkness. Our boys were roughhousing around the dug out when we suddenly heard a sickening thud. As turned on my heels, I realized that one boy had hit another player in the head with an aluminum bat. Billy and I reached the injured boy, and I expected his brains to be oozing from a fracture in his skull. To the contrary, the dazed boy sat on the ground and laughed about the entire incident. That year we began with a total lack of talent except for a few of the boys, Dallas and William being two of them, but by the end of the season, something bigger than us took over the team and guided and guarded it through the summer. The boys had a good baseball summer, and Dallas actually looked forward to playing the games.

WHO'S YOUR DADDY?

The year that the saying "Who's your daddy?" became popular was also the best year of Dallas's baseball career. However, things didn't start that way. In fact, the season began to look as if it would be a total failure.

Billy had taken on the job as the fourteen-year-olds' coach for the Knoxville Dodgers. Dallas, of course, was present at the tryouts, and he performed well enough to be chosen as a member of this team. Indeed, he was a strong first baseman who was developing his abilities to hit and pitch. Too, Billy knew and loved Dallas, and he wanted my son as a part of his team.

Dallas and I were both pleased that he found a team so early, especially since the off-season months had been spent taking more ground balls and swinging the bat. Now I could work him harder on those things, as well as on his pitching, instead of chasing teams and tryouts. Dallas wanted to relax since he made the team and just spend time being a kid, but I prevailed and forced him into those almost daily practices. I could see his increasing unhappiness with me, something that bordered on hate, but I was so consumed with making sure that my son was the absolute best player that he could be and hopefully the best one on the team that I ignored the warning signs.

One evening not too long after the team tryout with the Dodgers, Billy came to the house. His serious look immediately alerted me to the presence of some problem. As we always had done, we sat under the carport at the house so that he could dip his Skoal and I could smoke my cigarette. As soon as we reached the seats, Billy began,

"I've got some bad news to tell you, and I don't know what you're going to think about it or about me when I tell you. You might not want anything else to do with me, and I wouldn't blame you. Dallas can't play on this Dodger team that I'm coaching."

I sat in stunned silence. My mind wouldn't allow me to comprehend what Billy had just said. More to the point, I couldn't believe that Dallas was being done in again in baseball. My senses returned in the form of pure fury.

"What the hell do you mean he can't play for them? He went through the tryout, and you know as well as I do that he outplayed every other kid for his position. He hit the ball too. Why can't he play with them now?"

Billy began the explanation.

"Do you remember the guy who coached with the Powell team when we had the argument and near-fight during fall ball when the boys were twelve? Well, the assistant coach is the president of the Dodger Baseball Organization. He came to me after the tryouts and told me that under no condition could Dallas play for any Dodger team as long as he was in charge of the organization."

Billy looked at me to see if I was at the point of explosion and then continued.

"Joe, the guy is holding a grudge over the mess from that incident in fall ball. He is getting back at you through Dallas."

The anger began to rise, and I could feel the physical changes that occurred inside me. My blood pressure must have been close to stroke level.

"Billy," I bit off, "Tell the son of a bitch that I'll not go to any games if he leaves Dallas alone and lets him play for you. I'll do that with no questions asked. It's not fair to beat up Dallas because the guy doesn't have the guts to deal with me like a man!"

Billy answered,

"I've already tried everything to get the man to change his mind, but he won't budge. And don't tell me you can go a whole season without watching Dallas play. That isn't fair to you or to him."

"What the hell am I supposed to do, then?" I shouted.

Billy answered,

"There's still plenty of time to find another team for Dallas. I'll keep my ears opened for other teams and put in a good word for him. He's too good not to make a team."

"There's not much choice, is there?" I sniped.

Billy's last words were, "Man, I'm sorry." I could see in his face and hear in his voice the regret he had over the situation and the strain he felt growing in our friendship.

My mind was on something different than our friendship at the moment. I knew that somehow it would survive this latest crisis. What concerned me was the boy in the house. I had to tell him he'd been thrown off another team. Again, the reason that he was suffering during baseball season had nothing to do with his abilities. No, once again, his dad, the man who was supposed to be his biggest fan and supporter, had done him in. My actions had forced him off a team made up of many of his friends. His baseball abilities weren't in question. What was screamed in my face was the fact than no one wanted Dallas on the team because no one wanted to deal with me. I caused too many problems.

Worse, I couldn't see or accept that fact. I could only believe that I should continue to fight for Dallas, that I had his best interest in mind. Yet, every time I tried to help him, I actually hurt him. I made him a pariah.

Billy left, and I went to Dallas' room. There I told him about his being kicked off the team. His eyes welled up with tears, but at the same time he said,

"Don't worry about it, Dad. I didn't want to play for Billy and that team anyway. Well find another one."

I left his room, made my way back to the carport, and in the dark I broke down. I cried as my emotions flowed from anger to shame to regret. I said prayers to ask for guidance and to help make me a better dad and baseball parent. I pleaded for help so that I could quit caring so much about the game, Dallas' playing time, and his success.

Almost immediately, I began to search the sports section of the Sunday papers. The "Bulletin Board" listed teams who were to hold tryouts. I found one that was to audition prospective players on the coming Saturday. Dallas was shy about trying out in front of strangers, so once again, I pushed him to go. He grudgingly obliged me.

That Saturday we arrived at the park and waited in the car for people to show up. Dallas had learned long ago that my being on time meant arriving places at least fifteen minutes early. As we sat, I reminded Dallas of all the things on which he needed to concentrate in order to have a successful tryout. Not once did I consider that my jabbering might cause him to be nervous. I was already nervous enough for both of us. Too, Dallas still wore an apathetic expression when I talked baseball.

Boys began to arrive, and Dallas and I found the coach, Buddy McGee. He was a neat man with black hair and only a few flecks of gray, and he sported a mustache. He sent Dallas out to warm up with the other boys while I filled him in about Dallas' baseball history. He politely listened as I told him that Dallas was a second baseman, a first baseman, and a pitcher. My message came across loud and clear: Dallas could do everything.

I began my ritual of pacing. During any game or tryout, the soles of my shoes thinned as I walked. I smoked and smoked. I hid that from Dallas, even though he knew that I was a tobacco user. By the end of the event, my body collapsed in near exhaustion. Dallas never worked any harder than I did during those times.

Dallas had competition at second base. I boy named Mattie stood only five feet tall, yet he was catlike in his quickness. I fretted that Dallas wouldn't find much playing time at that position, but first base was a different story altogether. The one boy who played there was weak in his fielding and catching. His greatest attribute was his speed. However, Dallas possessed quickness from side to side, and his eye-hand coordination was second to none.

During the batting portion of the tryout, Dallas hit some balls. He had always been a pull hitter, and he continued that trend during his turn. Buddy had told the boys that he wasn't worried about whether or not they hit any ball; instead, he was watching the mechanics of their swings. That statement made Dallas and his dad a bit more comfortable.

Dallas was invited back to the second day of tryouts, and he made the team. He became a member of the Diamondbacks. Their colors were purple and gold, like LSU. I was proud of Dallas, and he seemed happy, except for the fact that he didn't know any of the boys. They were school friends, so I told Dallas that he would have to mingle and get acquainted, something that never came easy for him.

Dallas began the season as a second-string first baseman and pitcher. Soon, however, he won the starting position at first, something which infuriated the other boy and his parents but delighted me. Buddy worked the boys hard during practices, but some of them never worked to their full potential. We also had holes in the team that weakened it. As the season rolled along, the boys played better as a team, and they won most of their games.

Dallas played hard so that the other boys wouldn't think he didn't belong on the team and so that he might win their respect enough to become friends. As often happens with boys that age, friendships come quickly, as do hostilities. A couple of boys on the team and Dallas never got along, but they didn't take problems onto the field.

Buddy McGee was the best coach Dallas ever had, including Billy and me. Most likely, he reached my son because, unlike Billy or me, no emotional ties between them existed. He worked with all of the boys, and he had a style that made boys want to do well. Sometimes Buddy joked with a boy as a means of helping him. At other times, he fussed at them. On a few occasions he pulled them from games. Buddy had played ball during his high school years, and he was a natural athlete. Those things gave him credibility with the team and the necessary qualities to be a good leader.

Buddy's only shortcoming was that he was too hard on his son. Adam was a well-built athlete who played third base and pitched. When he was in a groove, he could mow batters down. However, he tended to let a mistake eat at him until his performance suffered. The entire time Buddy was fussing at Adam or giving him instructions. I could see and understand this flaw in Buddy, as well as in other dads, but I wouldn't admit the same thing about myself. Yet, everyone but me knew that I was an overbearing dad who needed to ease up on his son.

That year I let go of things for the first time. I had no control, but I still loosened my imaginary grip. Being one of the parents was fun. I enjoyed the moms and dads, and our trips to tournaments were fun as well.

Some of Dallas' best memories came that year. At a state-qualifying tournament in Kingsport, Dallas hit a shot to left field. On any regulation-sized field he would have hit a home run, but this field was home to the minor league team, and the walls were much deeper. During one league game at Levi Field in Powell, Dallas smacked a ball into left-center field. The hit was one that was bound for the fence as soon as the bat made contact. However, the umpire called the hit a ground-rule double. I was incensed that he had taken the home run away from Dallas. Fans who were walking to another field via our outfield fence indicated to the umpire that the ball had cleared the fence, but the ump wouldn't change his mind. Dallas and I still count that as the first and only home run in his career. After the season, Dallas gave me that baseball on which he had scribbled,

Home run # I

DB's vs. Panthers

9-6

6-11-99

Dallas Rector

Without a doubt, that ball is one of the most precious possession that I have today. Yes, I cried when he gave the ball to me. I knew deep down inside my heart what a jerk I had been to Dallas all of those years, and I felt shame. I didn't know how to stop, and I was afraid that if I let up he wouldn't put forth the effort necessary to be a high school ballplayer.

Two other coaches were Jeff Wells and Ronnie Fritts. Ronnie's youngest son Wesley provided countless hours of laughter for Dallas. He was only four or five at the time, but he loved baseball better than most of the boys on the team. He also could change the sound of his voice from a high-pitch to low and rough one. Wesley would make the change when a good play had been made or a strong hit had been delivered and would yell,

"Who's your daddy?"

Everyone in the bleachers, from both teams, and the players always burst into fits of laughter. Wesley helped to make the season fun.

That year's team was not the best one on which Dallas ever played. It was, however, the one that showed Dallas and me what baseball was supposed to be like, and we spent the rest of his career trying to find that feeling again. It didn't happen, but God bless Buddy McGee, Jeff Wells, and Ronnie Fritts. I'll always appreciate what they gave us

HIGH SCHOOL FALL BALL

During the fall before Dallas' freshman year, he played fall ball with boys in the grade above him. Their dads were the coaches, so he knew his playing time would be limited. Two boys played first in most games, and Dallas got the chance on rare occasions to play an inning or two. His batting was not spectacular, mostly because he was intimidated by high school pitchers. Everything was new to him, especially the speed of the game. Still, he hit as well as boys who had a year's experience in high school. At times Dallas wondered out loud why he even bothered to go to games since he didn't play that much. I told him that he was part of the team and that's the reason he had to go. I never considered whether or not my son even wanted to play high school ball. If he quit fall ball, I felt sure that he would never make the high school team in the spring. However, I made sure for the next three falls that Dallas would be involved in plenty of games. I asked for and was granted permission to be the coach of the fall ball teams on which he played. Of course, my son was anything but pleased with the prospects of going back to "normal."

One person can't coach a team, and luckily my nephew Brandon worked with the boys that first fall. Brandon had always played baseball full throttle, and he expected no less from this team. On more than one occasion he lined the boys up and had them run sprints after games. He did so as punishment for their half-hearted efforts. Dallas complained that he was getting fired upon from two fronts now. Brandon demanded that Dallas hustle at all times. No, he couldn't run fast, but Brandon required him to run through the base. I attacked him in the car, at home, and even in the dugout. The boy never got a break, and it's a wonder he didn't pack his bags and run away from home to escape the endless haranguing.

Brandon was "old-school" in baseball thinking. He insisted that Dallas slap tag any runner on first who dove back to the bag on a throw over by the pitcher. After several tries, Dallas began popping people with his glove when they dove back, and his action had the desired result: boys shortened their leads on pitchers so they wouldn't be beaten about the head and shoulders by the first baseman's mitt. In one particular game Dallas slapped a diving player. He rose to his feet and told Dallas,

If you hit me like that again, I'll whip your ass!

Dallas ignored the boy, and when he dove toward the base on the next throw, Dallas popped in the head with the glove. The boy glared at him but did nothing other than shorten the lead he took.

Brandon also believed in running the bases. He told the boys that the team would attempt to steal bases as often as possible. He also told them not to feel bad about being thrown out; he would have them steal the very next time they reached base. Aggressive plays made other teams make mistakes. It also frustrated other teams whose talents were superior to ours. Our players were like gnats that swarm and aggravate a person.

Those better teams might have prevailed in the end, but they were frustrated to the point of wanting to fight during the games.

My role during this season was to keep up with the paperwork. Brandon and his friend Travis coached the teams. Those high school boys loved playing the game that fall, and they would have run through brick walls for their young coaches, but not for me.

The second fall Brandon was unable to coach, so the job became mine. Travis again helped. We played in the Oak Ridge fall league, and several of the teams were loaded. One handicap that we faced was many of our players were involved with football during the fall. We had to adjust the team and cover positions with some second-string players and junior varsity players. The same core of boys played, but they didn't have the same faith in my abilities as they had in Brandon's. The players fell into old habits that hurt their performances. All the while, I pushed Dallas to continue to do what he knew was fundamentally sound. He stopped having fun, and then he began to gripe. My temper exploded, and I tore into him for his lousy attitude and his lack of effort. I told him, too, that I didn't appreciate his failure to show me the respect that he would show any other coach. He looked at me, but I could tell that he wasn't hearing a word I said. Of course, that infuriated me even more. That season ended with our team winning few games, and we were trounced by two of the top teams that in the spring would be among the best in the state.

The last year of fall ball was again fun. Jonathan, another young man and former player at the school, helped me as a coach. His personality was such that he easily got along with the boys. In fact, he kept them loose by joking and laughing with them. Dallas and his classmates were seniors now, and they had enough members on the team to tell what kind of season the spring would be. Most of the boys worked on their individual performances, and they found ways to have fun. However, one night circumstances turned the game into another nightmare.

We were playing another team from the west side of town. Dallas was pitching, and the game was fairly tight. Over the years Dallas had grown comfortable when he threw the ball inside, something Brandon had drilled into him to do. He told Dallas that each batter was fighting him for control of the plate. Dallas had to throw inside to show these players that the inside was his territory.

A batter from the other team crowded the plate, and Dallas threw inside. The ball clanked off the boy's batting helmet, and he immediately fell to the ground. Dallas looked horrified. He never tried to hit players, and having hit one in the head unnerved him. In later years the boy and Dallas attended the same college in Chattanooga. He told Dallas that the pitch had knocked him down and out.

When the boy went down, I looked to the other team's dugout on the first base side, and the fence gate wildly swung open. The dad of the boy who was hit charged the field. He was walking toward Dallas and freely throwing profanities his way as he threatened to stomp Dallas. As soon as I saw the man begin to yell at my son, I zipped out of the dugout, grabbed a bat, and made my way toward him. The entire time I was screaming,

You son of a bitch! Leave him alone. It was an accident. Don't get near him or I'll beat out your brains!

Again, I had lost my composure, but this might have been the one time in baseball when I was justified. No man was going to jump my son. He probably would have tattooed my face with his fists, but I wasn't going to allow the bully to pick on Dallas.

When the boy was helped to the dugout, the game continued, but after only one batter, I knew that Dallas couldn't pitch any more. I brought in a sophomore pitcher as relief. His warm-up gave an indication of things to come. His first pitch was high and outside—high enough to hit the top of a fifteen-foot tall backstop and outside enough so that the catcher could only retrieve the ball after it bounced off the wire enclosure.

The rest of the season the boys played for themselves. No, they didn't have fun, but at least Dallas had the opportunity to work on his game, and I had the chance to coach him one last time. Now he would have the winter to rest and fine-tune his skills.   Brandon continued to work with Dallas and his batting. They worked that winter in our basement. We hung a net from the floor joists, and Brandon spent hours running Dallas through drills. The boy must have swung at thousands of balls during soft-toss drills. Brandon taught Dallas to hit up the middle, pull the ball, and go with the pitch in order to hit it to the opposite field. By the time spring tryouts began, Dallas could hit the ball to all parts of the field. His one weakness occasionally reared its ugly head. He still struggled with off-speed pitches.

CAMP OF CHAMPIONS

During the summer some coaches ran summer baseball camps for players. The cost for admission was $100, too large a chunk of money for us to pay. Besides, the camps were for older boys, middle school and high school. That didn't make a difference to me.

The camp I wanted Dallas in was the Camp of Champions. Dwight Smith was a high school coach who organized the staff. He brought in other high school coaches from the area, as well as college coaches from the southeast and even a couple of professional players.

Dallas was about ten when I began working on the camp with Dwight. He needed someone to take over for my brother Jim, who'd been in charge of publicity and paperwork for earlier camps. I volunteered under the conditions that Dallas be allowed to go to camp with the other boys. That he was much younger and smaller never occurred to me. Dallas needed the instruction that would come from such a talented collection of coaches, and to tell the whole truth, I thought he might impress some college coaches who might remember him a few years down the road.

I recruited more than one hundred boys for the camp, and Dallas was in like Flint. On the first day we drove up, and I urged Dallas to listen carefully and give his best efforts every time. He verbalized his fears of playing with bigger guys, but I cut him short and told him to get tough. I never considered what a hard hit ball might do to a boy who was so much smaller and weaker.

Dallas instantly made friends with the coaches, and to this day he still enjoys seeing them and talking about ball and old times. Friends or not, the men coached Dallas and demanded the best from him. Unlike me, they were quick to praise good plays and were light in criticisms of the bad ones.

My son took his place in line during fielding exercises. When he was up, he tried to make plays, but too many times, the balls were hit too hard for little legs to reach them. That meant do-overs, so that by the time he went to the back of the line, he'd done two or three to every one the big guys did. He ran out of steam and couldn't catch up.

At breaks I walked to him and insisted that he pick up the energy and effort. Instead of telling me that he couldn't do it, Dallas listened to me and then turned and headed back to the field. He never spoke or whined.

He completed every drill and enjoyed the sliding station. There a large tarp was spread across the ground where boys started at a first base position and sprinted to second. When they reached a set point, they dropped and slid into the base. To make it easier and to cool boys from the sweltering conditions of summer days, a hose sprayed water on the tarp, and that allowed boys to slide and play at the same time. They looked as if they were speeding along on a Slip-and-Slide. It was one of the few times I saw Dallas smile during camp or game.

When we returned home, Dallas headed for his room. He closed the door and turned on his television. Later I would peak in and find him fast asleep. He would sleep away the afternoons and then be unable to sleep during the night, all of which made rising early for the next day's camp more terrible. His happiest day of the week was the last one, and he showed more energy getting out of the car when we arrived home on that day than he showed throughout the week.

Dallas attended the camp from then until his senior year. After that, he never missed the workouts and brutal heat, even though the camp improved his skills as a player.

I expected Dallas to take the things he learned at camp and to apply them to games. A crow hop, tossing the ball underhanded on a double play ball, getting a good lead off first were things I wanted him to do in live action, but I didn't get the fact that just learning them didn't mean he could perform them without plenty of practice. My badgering him to incorporate what he did in camp only made his game suffer. He was trying to please, but when he didn't, I fussed enough so that he just quit trying. Eventually those things became a part of his play, and then I'd lecture him about how well he played when he did them and that he shouldn't have defied me for so long.

On days when games weren't scheduled, I coaxed or brow beat Dallas into working on things in the evening. He'd had a belly full of baseball, but I told him the more he practiced, the better he'd become at using skills. In all honesty, he didn't care that much to improve because I was so avid. If I had been smart enough to back off, Dallas would have done things on his own and enjoyed the entire process more.

ROOKIE

Dallas began high school in 1999, and his work to make the high school team started almost immediately. He struggled through the first fall league and thought he'd have some down time, but after its season ended, the workout schedule began.

The high school coach expected every prospective player to attend weight training sessions, and Dallas realized that he would never be able to skip one of them unless he were on his deathbed. I taught in the same school, and I was pushing again about performing at his top level at all times because the coach might be watching. I quizzed him every day about the amount of weight he used in his exercise, and I asked him if he could increase it on any of his exercises. Dallas gave me a look as if to say,

"I'm busting my ass to be on this team. I workout as hard as any other guy. When is it good enough, Dad?"

I was blind to how he felt. My energies were too entwined in his making the team. Billy and I had talked over our sons' chances of making the high school team, and Billy assured me that they would do so with little problem. He even speculated on how they might move up to the varsity before the season was over. I disagreed with his assessment and told him that we needed to be happy if they received any playing time at all.

In addition to the workouts with the team, I forced Dallas to work on his hitting every Sunday night. We met Billy and William, and for the next two or three hours, Dallas split time with William swinging at baseballs thrown by a pitching machine. The machine was set to throw pitches in the eighty mile per hour range, and I expected Dallas to hit the ball every time. When he struggled, I stopped him and discussed the flaws in his mechanics. He listened not at all.

I hired the son of the high school's former baseball coach to give Dallas hitting lessons. For two years, Shane worked with Dallas, and he made giant strides in his abilities to hit. If Shane said it was right, then Dallas did all within his power to complete the task. Dallas took all of Shane's ranting and raving with no ill effects. The difference, Dallas said, was that Shane had been there, he understood what it was like. The boy took an imaginary swing below the belt and racked his dad mightily. They met in a converted hay barn owned by the dad of an upperclassman on the team. The place was damp and raw in the cold weather, but I told Dallas to just put on an extra layer of clothing and to get busy.

When tryouts were held in January and February, I was not a person around whom most people wanted to spend time. I knew that Dallas would make the team as a courtesy from one faculty member to another. My sights were already set higher. I wanted Dallas to work hard enough to become the starting first baseman on the junior varsity team. He was equal to the others on the team, but he was a year younger than they were, and as a result, he played sparingly. However, when he did gain an opportunity, he made the best of the chance. Dallas fielded ground balls with ease, and he hit with surprising power. On those occasions I stood with my chest stuck out and an extra bounce was in my steps. I would give Dallas a big hug and smile, but he wasn't buying into it. I had on too many previous occasions acted the same way, only to drop bombs of criticism on him later in the evening.

Still, my son saw the field all too little in my opinion. The boys ahead of him weren't better; they were older. The first baseman was a good pitcher, but he was too stiff to play the infield position. Dallas found a true friend in his JV coach that year, and they enjoyed hamming it up before and after games. Scott used Dallas as a pitcher on occasion. I traveled to each and every game that year, and although I was disappointed at his lack of playing time, I assumed that the situation was only for one year. In fact, when the sophomore players moved up to the varsity during the year, my heart skipped with excitement because I realized that more playing time for Dallas was coming. Wrong! The boys who moved up sat with the varsity and played most of the JV games as well, at least for a while.

At the end of the season a junior varsity tournament was held at fields in Oak Ridge, the site of the creation of the first atomic bomb. Dallas saw spurts of action. He pitched, played first, and pinch-hit. I was glad to see him on the field, especially since I knew how hard he had worked in the off-season to prepare himself. I constantly badgered him to ask if he was discouraged, so much so that I eventually made him that way. He would tell me over and over again,

"Dad, I'm fine about my playing time. I'm a freshman, and I'll get my chance after I've paid my dues. I just like being on the team so that I play some. Relax!"

The biggest ballgame during Dallas' freshman year was against Clinton High School. For years Dallas had played with and against one of the other school's most highly praised ball players, Matt Patterson. Dallas didn't especially get along with the boy, most of all because Matt picked at weaker, smaller kids. That included most of the boys in his age group. Granted, Matt could hit the ball a ton, and he was a decent pitcher. However, even he admitted that he had *hands of stone*. A ball stood a fifty-fifty chance of being caught by the boy. He loped through the outfield like a gazelle, but when he reached the ball, Matt was sometimes as clumsy as a newborn calf.

On this night Matt pitched for Clinton, and Dallas, as well as his dad, was nervous about his performance. His time at bat arrived, and Dallas stepped into the box. The two boys looked at each other and grinned. That was perhaps the best thing about playing open league ball. Boys met others from all areas of the county or from completely different counties or cities. The longer they played against each other, the better they knew one another and the more respect they held for each other. Sometimes a lifelong friend was made as the result of playing on a team.

Parents were no where near as kind. An unhealthy hate among adults of different teams grew. We were so wrapped up in winning and in our sons' performances that none of us gave thought to the event being just a game. No, it was some monumental moment that defined our sons' lives and futures. And each time they played, the same feelings emerged. Not one parent was close to being as mature and wise as his or her son.

Dallas called for time as he dug his right foot into the dirt. He then relaxed into his batting stance, the one on which I had worked him so many hours for so many years, the one that Shane and his cousin Brandon taught him in one lesson.

Matt knew that Dallas struggled with off speed pitches, and he tried a couple on him, but Dallas didn't go fishing by reaching for a bad pitch. He sat back and waited, and sure enough, Matt released a smoking fastball. Dallas uncoiled and met the ball at the perfect time. Its flight in the night sky caught the attention of every person in the park. I knew the ball had a chance of being a home run and so did Dallas. As fate worked, the ball hit the top pole running horizontally along the fence. As if to show the crowd that it had a mind of its own, the ball chose to bounce in play instead of on the other side of the fence. Dallas missed a home run by an inch, literally.

He had taken on Matt one-on-one and had won that time. The occasion was special because Dallas' sister, Lacey, and her fiancé, Nick, drove from Murfreesboro to watch the game. The boy who had been robbed of a home run stood on second base with a broad grin on his face. Matt turned to look at him and smiled and showed the dimples on his face. That night Dallas performed for his family and earned the respect of a former foe. Most of all, my son learned that he could play this game with abilities that equaled those of most boys against whom he competed.

Being on this team was also special because a new high school field had been built. The old one was located about a mile from the high school and was plowed under when the middle school expansion occurred. One of my hopes was that Dallas would be able to play high school ball on that old field. It was a much better field than the new one. The former baseball coach had scratched the red clay soil and shale of East Tennessee long hours to produce a lush Bermuda grass infield and a green, thick outfield. The new ballpark stood as a monument to making mistakes. The principal of the school insisted upon being the construction leader, especially after thousands of dollars were spent to dig and haul dirt. When the principal was named director of construction, most of the money had already been spent. His goal was to finish the field with what funds were left. Still, he was a basketball man whose contact with a ball field was mostly confined to playing men's softball. The former baseball coach wanted to take on the project so that the facility would be a showcase. Instead, the plot of ground was a constant headache. The entire area was sloped incorrectly, so any rainwater on the field ran toward home plate and first base. Home plate was placed in the west corner of the field, and during spring games, the entire defensive team stood squinting into a blinding sun as baseball zipped off aluminum bats and toward their bodies. Pitchers were especially susceptible to being tagged by a pitch hit back at them. At times, they couldn't see the ball being thrown back to them by their own catchers.

The principal also decided where the dugouts were to be placed. Surrounding the home plate area was a block wall three or four feet high. Pads covered the top portions of this wall, but any baseball that hit the bottom had the same movement as a pinball. This wall was no more than twenty feet from the plate, so a runner had little chance of advancing to another base even when the ball escaped the catcher's grasp. An expansive net stretched around the area above the wall to catch foul balls.

Down the base lines the dugouts were set. The visiting teams sat on the first base side, and our team sat on the third base side. Behind the visitors' dugout was a small walk, and beyond it a steep bank almost barren of any grass ran to parking lot of several small businesses. Behind the home dugouts an equipment barn sat, and unfinished warm-up pitching mounds were located halfway down the left field line. Behind the ball field on this side was a field of wheat sometimes and silage corn during other years. Baseballs fouled in either direction were difficult to retrieve, especially during night games.

The ridiculous aspect of these dugouts was that they were built into the fences that ran down either outfield line. Fans who sat anywhere other than immediately behind home plate missed parts of the games as they unsuccessfully craned their necks to see around those small enclosures for players. The principal wanted all the rooflines to be the same as the ones on the football field, so the jutting angles of these roofs only made a terrible sightline worse.

The best seats in the park were in right field. One set of bleachers was placed there, and Billy and I unofficially claimed them as ours. Not many folks sat there because few baseball parents liked Billy or, more correctly, me enough to sit with us. Having the entire set of bleachers gave us the opportunity to discuss plays and coaching strategies. Too, plenty of time was spent reminiscing about earlier days that we coached together and the stunts we pulled.

Whoever surveyed the field did so with a defective instrument because the drop from the outfield to first base was a disastrous two feet. Every rain that passed over swamped the right side of the infield with run-off water. The outfield, however, didn't give up all of its moisture. Boys played many games in two or three inches of standing water. A dive for a sinking fly ball required a face mask and air tank as water splashed heavenward. The worry about injuries to players was overshadowed with concern about their possible drowning.

This, then, was the "million dollar" baseball field that received so much attention during its construction period. Visiting fans looked on in amazement at the poor condition of the field. The grass on the outfield resembled that of any cow field in the county. The infield, consisting of Bermuda sod that was laid by parents and players, never filled in because the coach didn't keep it watered and he cut it with a John Deere tractor and bush hog or belly mower. The coach never aerated the field or spread sand to allow the creepers from the Bermuda grass to spread. Weeds grew around the warning track that was weeded during the pre-season and then never touched until the next season.

My free period during the school year was the last one of the day. I felt an obligation to help the coach with the field whenever he needed me. Wet days found me on that field at 2 p.m., and I didn't leave until 10 that night. We raked; pumped, swept, and squeegeed gallons of water; and poured hundreds of wheelbarrows filled with sand and Turfus onto the infield dirt to make it playable for the games. I also helped him in developing a constitution and by-laws for a booster club. It protected the coach in every way and prevented parents from running roughshod over him. I never regretted helping with creating ground rules by which the organization operated. As a teacher and former coach, I had witnessed plenty of situations where overeager parents tried to ramrod things past the coach.

I freely admit that I did some of this to enhance my son's chances of playing when he reached the varsity level. This coach rarely stayed for junior varsity games, so he had little first-hand knowledge as to who could and couldn't play. Anything that might get Dallas an extra look was what I sought. Yet, I worked on Saturdays and during my free periods because I loved being involved with the game and the team in some way. Of course, as soon as Dallas walked on the field for practice or games, I walked off of it.

The best thing about this year was the souvenir baseball that Dallas received at the first game played on the new field. Otherwise, the season was spent with Dallas' playing role being minor and my involvement and invested time being large.

SOPHOMORE MISERY

Dallas' second year of high school continued his misery. He once again had attended every workout and had lifted weights, a fact I can personally attested to after he swept into the kitchen one day, whisked me off my feet, and squeezed the air from my lungs with a crushing bear hug that was meant to be loving. Dallas had reached the age that all boys reach when they must prove their strength. Strapping young males then play games with their fathers that are actually contests where the leadership of the pride is determined. On that day when Dallas damn near caved in my ribs and punctured my lungs, he came close to being the dominant male, but I wasn't ready to let go of my position yet. I growled something about his not wanting me to unleash a pound of "whip-ass" on him. He smiled, let me go, and waited. It was a bluff, and he knew it.

During this off-season I did insist that he work on his hitting even more. Billy had opened up his own version of a baseball academy earlier, and as such,

Dallas had open use of the batting cages. At least a couple of times each week we made the twelve-mile drive to Oak Ridge, where Dallas swung a bat until his hands blistered. He complained about the pain, but I showed little sympathy. The blisters that I had earned at his age came from work either at home or on some summer job. I well knew that those blisters would heal and that calluses that would never fail him when he needed most to grip the bat would replace them. Besides, the only blisters I ever earned in sports were the ones that formed on by butt from having to "ride the pine."

I then made Dallas work on his pitching; he threw approximately fifty pitches each night that we went to the facility. Most were fastballs, but he also threw a few curve balls and a few change-ups. His best pitch was a dropping change-up. It bent a bit, and then as if the bottom fell out, the ball sank straight into the dirt. The pitch was so nasty that I implored him to use it more. I pushed Dallas because I believed that the chance for him to play varsity ball was strong.

Again, he made the team, a foregone conclusion by everyone. In fact, Dallas was named the starting first baseman. Other boys who were a year older than he still played some games on junior varsity because they simply were not good enough to play up. So, the head coach dictated to his assistant that these boys be given playing time in front of Dallas. At that point the misery began in earnest. As a father I was incensed. My son sat behind these boys the year before as they played. Now when Dallas was supposed to play, he was again being benched so that boys who weren't good enough to play on the varsity were allowed to hang on by competing in games with younger, smaller players.

The coach loved the players whose class preceded Dallas'. They were the first boys that he worked with upon becoming a coach at the school. A few of them possessed some talent, but the overall opinion was that the class was weak. Still, the coach held special places in his heart for each boy, and he gave them extra playing time which they didn't earn and which they could not athletically handle. While the coach coddled this group and their parents, he berated or ignored completely the boys behind them.

Dallas was chosen sometime after the season began to dress with the varsity. He still played on the junior varsity team, but he also had the chance to play with "the big boys," or so we all thought. Most of his time with the varsity consisted of chasing down foul balls that rolled down the hills on either side of our field. The hill behind the first base dugout was a severe slope. It was a sprawling red clay mud pit whenever the slightest amount of rain fell. Behind the third base line was a farmer's field that was each season thick with vegetation. Dallas returned from ball hunts either caked in mud or congested and sneezing from pollen. His playing time was minimal, if not totally absent. Alas, Dallas became little more than a glorified ball boy for the team.

Billy was furious because William was not selected to dress with the varsity. He vowed that William was finished and that he would transfer to Oak Ridge for his last two years of ball. I tried to talk him out of the move, but he was too thoroughly disgusted with what he perceived as the coach's slight of his son. After ten years of playing ball together, Dallas and William would be completely separated, and I worried for myself and about being able to maintain my ties to my best friend.

The team did take a trip to the Nashville area for a tournament. Dallas warmed up every game; he stretched, ran, and threw as if he were going to play a tremendous amount. In reality, he spent most of his time rubbing the numbness from his bottom that came from long sitting stints on the bench. For the entire tournament, he pinch-hit in one game where the issue of the win was already determined. The coach had him bat cold, no swings of preparation, no mental adjustments. The man on the mound threw pure heat and Dallas was quickly dispensed to the dugout. He might have played an inning or two in the last game of the weekend, but again, the outcome was already decided. In short, he and I had wasted time and money for this trip. Also lost that weekend was a little more of my son's confidence and love for the game.

That season proved to be excruciating as one of life's lessons shook Dallas, his teammates, and parents to the core. The night was a cold one, brutally cold weather for a baseball game. Of course, any time we played ball at Halls High School, the weather turned unbearably frigid, the kind of cold that cuts through layers of clothes and settles into joints so that they ache like bad teeth. The game itself wasn't remarkable or memorable in any way. The boys finished the game, and Dallas and I began the long walk to the car. Suddenly, we heard screaming, and someone came rushing toward us babbling that Larry Dillon, the dad of one of Dallas' best friends on the team, had collapsed in the parking lot. I took off in a full sprint and arrived at the scene. One person was working with Larry, but the rest of the crowd stood in stunned disbelief. I knelt down and began immediately to administer mouth-to-mouth resuscitation. Each breath I blew into Larry's lungs rushed back out from a flapping of his lips. I looked into Larry's eyes as I continued the procedure, and they held that far away stare that told me that he was gone. Still, we worked with him until the emergency units arrived after what seemed like hours. No one wanted to believe that the life of a man who was so vibrant and jolly had suddenly ended.

My son stood stunned at the sight of someone he had known so long now lying lifelessly on the ground. I steered him toward the car, and we left immediately. On the way home, Dallas asked if we could go to the hospital, and I decided against it. He'd faced enough trauma for one day. Instead, I told him that we needed to touch base with Amy. I promised that I would go to the hospital as soon as we made the stop, but I persuaded him to stay at the house and contact friends that he and Larry's son Josh shared. Dallas agreed with my suggestion. I went alone to the hospital to check on Josh and his family.

Late that night I came home to tell Dallas what I had known since I tried to administer aid: Larry was dead the moment he hit the ground from a massive heart attack. Dallas cried only a bit, and then he informed me that his re-contacting players and friends was the most important thing he needed to accomplish.

That night showed me that many other things in this life are more important than baseball. Dallas had known this truth for some time; I was the slow one of the pair, and frankly, in relatively little time, I forgot the lesson. Before long, I once again was on the baseball parent trail as I coaxed and prodded and badgered my son into playing errorless ball when he got the chance.

During that year I heard the first rumblings of parents in regard to the coach and his dealings with parents. One boy and his mother in particular grew more and more disgruntled and hostile. Cancer had taken the life of the boy's dad, and the mother swore that the coach had promised the father on his deathbed that he would watch after the son. Instead, the boy became the target of the coach's wrath. He couldn't do a thing right. The coach demoted him until all he did was pitch an occasional inning and play outfield sporadically. The senior was a better than average ball player who needed some encouragement, not the tirades of a coach. As the season continued, this boy's interest in the team and sport eroded to the point that he prayed for the year to end so that he could escape the man who had become such a jerk. The mother was livid, and to this day she has never forgiven the coach nor forgotten how he treated her son.

I talked with the coach and tried to warn him of the impending firestorm. I never said a thing behind the man's back that I didn't say to his face. In the conversation, I explained that perceptions of parents might be wrong, but they were what remained true to them and were the things being reported to principals and other administrators. In fact, I actually told him that this mother was furious and that her son needed a bit of encouragement. Evidently, the man didn't take the advice I gave.

While the way that this boy was treated seemed unfair, I never imagined that the coach did, in reality, pick at him, not until other players made comments. If such treatment was obvious to the players, then the mother might have had reason to be so incensed.

Perhaps the most exciting event of Dallas' second year occurred one spring day in April. One of the local high schools had no field of its own, and it played home games for a season at what used to be Knoxville's minor league stadium. Several of today's great big league players, such as Todd Helton and Carlos Delgado, swung bats at Bill Meyer Stadium. In its background stood the old Standard Knitting Mill, where Knoxville at one time had the distinction of producing more underwear that any other U.S. city. Windows at the old plant had been shattered by countless baseballs on their screaming flights out of the park. Dallas was excited to be playing on a field with such rich history.

He stepped in for his first at bat during the game, and I detected the nervousness of my son as he vainly tried to find a comfortable place in the batter's box. I knew that he would strike out and would spend the rest of the game feeling that his performance was unbefitting this shrine. Then the opposition's pitcher tried to blow a fastball by Dallas. He didn't know any better. Dallas wasn't a great curve ball hitter, but a fastball on the inside corner of the plate was always *meant* for him. Dallas had a perfect swing that day. His bat met the ball, and he followed through completely. The ball exploded off his bat with one of those sounds that announces that a rocket has just been launched. Dallas should have run, but he watched the flight of the ball. No, it didn't clear the park, but it hit the top of the wall. Our hearts pounded, mine because my son had clobbered the ball and his because he had done himself proud in the old stadium.

The team struggled through district play and made an early exit from the tournament. Thankfully, the season was over. Dallas thought he could relax, but summer ball was just beginning, and he would have another horrible time.

Dallas played for the grandfather and uncle of one of the junior varsity boys. Zack was the same boy who played for Billy and me the in training league. He was the child who ran from third to second to field a ball. He was older now, but he still played the same wild, all-over-the-place game. William also played for these men. From the start the entire situation was a fiasco. Zack batted in the top of the order, a good thing due to his speed, but a bad thing since he rarely got a hit. Dallas, on the other hand, continued to make good contact and to deliver hits, but he was dumped to the seven-eight spots of the line-up. He couldn't do much for the team at the position.

Let's face it. I didn't have faith in many of the coaches for whom Dallas played. For some reason, I felt that they didn't know enough about the game or the boys to be successful. No, only I could coach those teams as they should be coached. I groused and complained about the way things were run. When Dallas got in the car after a ballgame, I critiqued the coaching. Then I picked apart each and every play that Dallas made or didn't make. The pressure from me was relentless.

After one game, I left aggravated at the turn of events. Again, we had lost the game, and Zack began his usual pouting and whining. I told him to *Shut up!* Lynn, his grandfather, came rushing from the crowd and stood in my face yelling,

Don't you talk to my grandson like that! I'll break your jaw! I'll break your jaw!

I took a step back and told him that I wasn't going to fight an old man, but he kept egging me on. Finally, I laid down my folding chair and turned back to meet him. I howled,

Fine old man. If you want to fight, I'll break you in half! I'll stomp you!

Dallas comes running up and grabs me. He implored,

Dad, it's not worth it. Let's just go home.

Again, another case emerged of the child being the adult. One of Dallas' best friends, Dustin Cline, was on the team, and he stills sends me messages and emails with the "I'll break your jaw" line. It's something about which we can laugh—now.

This team traveled to Nashville to play in one of the dozens of state tournaments. Its performances during those games were no different from the rest of the season. Dallas had gone on this trip because I made him. The boys played two and were through.

Finally, Dallas had a few weeks of peace that didn't include baseball or me. He lived the life of a normal sixteen-year-old boy. A part-time job gave him some spending money that he used on evenings out with friends. Baseball was in another universe as far as he was concerned, and he liked it that way.

JUNIOR INJUSTICES

Finally Dallas arrived at the first of his varsity years. He was a legitimate member of the varsity team as a pitcher and as a first baseman. Two senior boys stood in front of him at first, although neither played the position better. The coach told the boys, as he had told them each year, he intended to play the best person at the position, regardless of grade he was in. Once again, the man lied to the boys.

Dallas worked out with pitchers and catchers during the winter, and he spent time in the weight room to improve his strength. He endured the excruciating drills to improve agility and speed. Yes, Dallas bought the line that the coach fed him. He believed that he was on an equal basis with the other boys who were first basemen. However, he forgot that these boys were members of the group to whom the coach had always shown favoritism. Dallas was doomed from the start, but he didn't even know it.

One boy couldn't find a position on the team. In earlier years he had played the middle infield, but two other boys were securely entrenched in those positions. His throws were too erratic for him to be placed at third base. Inability to consistently catch a fly ball or stop a grounder kept him from breaking into the outfield line-up. So, the coach placed the boy on first. He possessed excellent speed, and sometimes he made good plays at the position, but he usually made one error that broke the team's collective back in most games. His batting skills were nonexistent. He struck out or hit weak grounders to infield players. The boy was blessed with blinding speed, but it was of no value because he was on base so seldom. Still, the coach stuck with him. Parents came to me during games and wondered aloud why Dallas sat the bench when he was the superior player. One of the dads made these feelings known to me, and I believed him because he had been a player, coach, and manager in the big leagues.

The other senior played sparingly at first. He was a better than average pitcher, but his hands turned to stone and his feet mired in quicksand the moment he stood on the field as the first baseman. This boy had good power in his bat and accumulated several hits during the season. Still, his forte was pitching. The coach realized how important this player's pitching was to the team, and he overused the boy to the point that he his arm was dead before the season ended. The movement on his fastball abandoned him, and without that movement, his best pitch became easy prey for opposing teams.

All the while, other boys, including Dallas, were able to pitch and to do so effectively. During the few chances that they received, they won games that weren't supposed to be victories. Dallas pitched in a tournament against a private school whose team was loaded with superb players. That night he shut the team down, and he earned an important and confidence-building win. For most of the season, the coach brought Dallas into games with bases juiced and the pressure palpable. Sometimes Dallas won the contest; sometimes he lost it. Still, he worked diligently because he still bought into the coach's promise to play the best players.

During the off-season Dallas had taken batting instruction from Brandon. Although he was a mere 5'6", Brandon had been a leader in home runs during his senior year, and he played college ball at two small schools. It was Brandon who taught Dallas that looking pretty when he swung the bat meant nothing if he didn't hit the ball with power. Brandon drilled into Dallas the idea that he should swing his bat with mean intentions and not worry about what he looked like to the crowd or other players. Dallas took the advice to heart, and he began crushing the ball. Several at-bats ended with the ball careening off the top part of the outfield fence. Sometimes he hit towering fly balls that were easy outs. Whenever he made contact, the ball rifled from his bat. Dallas was pleased with his production and felt sure that the coach would soon insert him into the starting rotation. Instead, the coach called Dallas to the side one game and told him,

You won't ever get a hit or be worth a dime until you quit swinging like Sammie Sosa and trying to hit everything out of the park!

This comment came from a man who NEVER played a day of college ball and who hit about a buck-eighty five during his glorious high school career. Of course, this criticism aimed at Dallas was given where everyone, players and fans, could hear. Instantly, Dallas' belief in himself bottomed out, and he then accepted the fact that he would never be the starting first baseman on the team. Even though the other boys weren't as good as Dallas, they were part of the coach's inner circle.

I witnessed the good and the bad of Dallas' game. I was still his biggest fan, but I was also his harshest critic. I growled at him about what I perceived to be his lack of hustle and his half-hearted efforts. At the same time, I was beginning to grow angry with the coach for his failure to play Dallas. The whisperings in my ears from other parents did little to quell my fury. I didn't confront the coach because I knew doing so would only hurt Dallas' chances more. I spent my time during games in the right field bleachers, and I grumbled loudly about my son being *screwed*. I am not proud of my failure to speak to the coach. Instead, I sounded like so many disgruntled parents who merely complain about how he ran the team. I felt that in doing so I was becoming like that dad whom I went after so many summers earlier.

Over spring break the team traveled to Myrtle Beach to play in a prestigious tournament. The coach promised the players that the tournament would be a time for them to have some fun and to also play ball. The prospects of Dallas' playing ball and our vacationing a few days on the beach excited Amy and me. She took a week of her vacation, we packed the car, reserved a motel room, and headed for fun in the sun. WRONG! The weather was cold, too cold to swim or enjoy walking on the beach for more than brief jaunts. Some of the boys, whose youthful bodies could stand the frigid temperatures, did play in the incoming waves, and others swam.

The tournament was an infuriating time for Amy and me. Dallas was put in as a pinch-hitter in the last inning of the first game. The opposing pitcher threw in the 90's, and Dallas was out before he warmed up. For the entire week,

Dallas played maybe five innings. Yes, the coach had promised playing time, but we believed that his statement meant more than five lousy innings. Amy wasted her vacation days, Dallas was in an emotional free-fall as he realized that he had been given the least playing time of anyone on the team, and I was so enraged that I began to make comments that I knew the coach could hear. I finally asked him why Dallas was receiving no playing time, but the coach ignored my question. To this day, I don't know what his reasoning was.

The trip home was long and torturous. I raged about the coach and made sure that my son knew he had been mistreated. I snapped at Amy and Dallas, and I was too mad to speak to the coach; glaring at him was the only thing I could effectively do. Dallas said nothing, and Amy sat quietly as I continued my tirade. I found out a year later just how mad she was.

The team returned home to finish the season. The first part of the year the team had met with unexpected success, but the second half was not nearly so positive. Games were lost to teams whom our boys should have beaten handily. Players who were in the game went through the motions and gave little, if any, effort. By the end of the season, our team had lost its once overwhelming lead in the district became the second place team.

The district tournament was played at the field of the district champion. This was the school from which our coach had graduated. In fact, his coach still ran the baseball program. Players and fans alike always felt that our coach didn't want to or didn't feel capable of beating his former coach. A win against them came on rare occasions, but the outcome was always in spite of our coach's efforts.

The first round of the tournament, our team was scheduled to play at 5 p.m. That night also was the evening of the senior prom. The seniors wanted to go to the prom, the only one they would ever attend, so the coach made his home available to his special boys. After the game he took them to his house where they could shower, dress, and leave to pick up dates on their ways to the prom. No such special consideration was ever given to Dallas and his friends the next year.

Those seniors came to the game not wanting to play, and I understood that. I was shocked when Dallas actually started at first base for the game. We lost to a team that we had beaten twice during the regular season, but this time our boys lost to superior coaching. Our leader seemed no more interested in the game than the seniors. The year ended with a whimper instead of the bang our coach had sworn he wanted. This group of boys played the entire season above their heads, and they had won many games that they should have lost. In the end, they proved to be the weak group of seniors that most of us realized they always had been. Only a couple of players were exceptions in this senior class.

To be able to say that baseball ended for the year would have been nice, but it didn't. Billy and I again put together boys who would be seniors the coming year. We joined a league that featured several excellent teams. We also had good players, and the games were played on the field of the defunct minor league Knoxville team. By this time, these boys knew every coaching line that Billy and I offered. So, we let them play. Billy again took the duties of the third base coach, and he gave complicated signs, all of which meant nothing. We used signs when we wanted a bunt, hit-and-run, and steal. Other than that, we allowed the boys to simply play.

I pushed Dallas to play well. Only parents and girlfriends attended these games, but I cajoled my son to work harder on his game. He needed to make sure that he stayed sharp for his senior season and any potential college coaches who might offer him a scholarship. His fielding continued to be stellar, and he averaged at least one hit every three at bats, but I wanted him to be on base every time. My stomach turned to a swarm of bees when he faced the best pitchers in the area because I wanted him to establish himself as someone whom they feared. Although Dallas racked up his share of hits, he never struck fear into those pitchers' hearts. The more I pushed, the less he listened until I gradually eased up in frustration on the fussing.

Even when I tried to avoid trouble and controversy, it stalked me and appeared at the worst of times. In a tournament in Jefferson County, a team that was inferior spanked us. The game was called early as the result of the slaughter rule. Our players came late to the ballgame and spent time goofing off instead of preparing mentally and physically. Billy couldn't be at the game, so I became the sole boss. I exploded with the entire team. I gave them the kind of tongue lashing that I served Dallas on a daily basis. We played the next day, and a different team showed up. Dallas pitched one of the games we played. He never pitched any better, nor did he ever look more like a man than he did on the mound that day. A snapshot of him showed his maturity and concentration. For one game, Dallas did what I knew he could do all along: play with any group of players his age. Our opponent was a team from Ohio, and they were cocky and undefeated. The boys went out and played as they were capable, and we beat the other team.

The end of the league season came, and our team was tied for first with another team. A tie-breaking game between us would decide who would go to the state tournament. The other team dominated us for most of the game. They did so with only nine players. At one point a player on our team and one for the Orioles fought. Both were ejected from the game, and because that left the Orioles with only eight players, they were forced to forfeit the game. As a result, our team was awarded the trip to the state tournament. I consoled the other team's players by telling them I was embarrassed and that they should be the ones going to the state. Of course, those words of consolation fell on deaf ears. Yet, for everything that folks might think of me, no one could ever call me a cheater.

Billy was also coaching his daughter's softball team during the summer, and they were going to Florida the same week. My wife was having surgery during that time and needed me at home while she recuperated, so I wasn't going to the tournament. Too, for the first time I didn't demand that Dallas go to a tournament. I knew that he struggled with some of the boys on this team, and he was better off staying home. He was working a summer job in order to have spending money for the summer and coming school year. Some of the other parents were livid that I refused to go on the trip, and I understand their feelings. However, my wife's health was more important than any ballgame. That's an amazing sentiment from someone who for so many years had been consumed by the sport. Some of the dads took over the coaching duties and took the team to Nashville. There they played two games, made a speedy exit, and returned home.

I knew that summer was the last one I would have with Dallas and baseball. I shed a few tears over that, but I also felt some of the crushing weight of baseball lifting from my shoulders. One more year of pushing and prodding and then Dallas could take care of any baseball after that. Next year, Dallas' senior year, would be the one I had always dreamed of. My son would be front and center as a starter on his high school team.

THE SENIOR SCREW

The year finally arrived. At last Dallas was the "king of the hill," the top dog who would be the first baseman for the high school team. He had more than paid his dues. Even though he was a better player than others, he had ridden the pine. Dallas worked during the other off-seasons and during the long days of spring practices, only to be denied the opportunities which the coach had given. Things would finally be better now that he would be playing consistently and be trying to demonstrate senior leadership.

The team's potential was undeniable. Boys had played together for several years. The infield was solid, and it even featured a boy who would become the starting shortstop during his freshman year at the University of Alabama. Although Dallas's speed still handicapped him, his quickness and his hand-eye coordination made him an excellent first baseman. One of his former instructors commented,

Dallas isn't the best player available. But he might be the smartest one. He has baseball intelligence from having been around the game so long. When you put that with his talents, a pretty good ball player is standing in front of you.

Another senior who had improved tremendously over his four years covered third base. His best play was charging a slow roller or bunt and making a pinpoint throw to first. Too, he had grown from a little guy to someone who hit with power. Josh had more than earned his spot. Yes, he had stuck with baseball even after his dad had died at a game a couple of years earlier.

Dallas also worked with the pitchers and catchers all winter. The speed on his pitches was not as impressive as their location. Throughout his baseball career he had won by putting the ball in the correct spot. However, his size and workouts had him throwing the ball a bit harder. His pitches included a fastball, a curve ball, and a change-up that fell straight to the ground and curved as it arrived at the plate. No, he couldn't blow folks away, but he could pitch effectively most of the time.

At times he wanted to miss a workout because he had too much homework or he wanted a life that included something other than baseball. I raged when he wanted those days off. I told him that he was letting himself and the team down when he missed. After harassing him so severely, he didn't dare miss a workout. Also, I told him that he might lose his position if he missed.

The two glaring weaknesses of the team were pitchers and outfielders. The pitching staff featured not one dominating person. Each boy could keep teams off stride, but they weren't the caliber of pitchers who could take over a game. The outfielders were, simply put, weak. Part of the problem was youth. Some of the better fielders made mistakes that young players normally make. The other part of the problem dealt with lack of talent. One senior player wasn't able to track a ball in the outfield. In fact, he couldn't do it when he was twelve years old. He was, however, fast and strong. Occasionally, his bat met the ball, and when the meeting occurred, the boy crushed the ball. I say the meeting was by chance because when he swung, his head came off the ball so much that he was looking at the stands over his left shoulder. Another boy was a transfer from out-of-state. He talked all fall about the success his former high school team had enjoyed the year before, and players, coaches, and parents were excited about his arrival. However, when he played in games, several things were obvious: he couldn't hit a curve ball, he couldn't judge a fly ball, he couldn't stop a ground ball, and he could barely throw the ball from right field to second base.

The pre-season began, and the team had good days and bad days. Yet, the potential of the boys was evident. During home games I continued to sit in the right field bleachers and separate from most fans. At away games I hung on fences as far away from the action as possible. Still, my loud, grating voice could be heard over everyone else's, and Dallas felt constant pressure from me. He also experienced the growing sense of disgust with me and all that I had done over the years.

The coach—what a lousy guy! The man was in his late twenties. His dad and the principal of the school were good friends, so when the position opened and he applied for it, the job was his. His experience in baseball amounted to having played high school baseball. His skills then were limited, and he was too young and inexperienced to be named a head coach. However, the man was an excellent game coach. He had a knack for calling the right play at the right time to win games.

What the coach lacked was people skills. I always enjoyed debating with him during the school year. He was a staunch Republican, and many were the times that we good-naturedly argued with each other about government programs. Yet, the man struggled to get along with parents and other adults. Part of the reason was that he told parents and players things and then arbitrarily changed his mind. To those people to whom he had made promises, his changes appeared to be the telling of lies. He refused to give an accounting for these changes, another thing that whipped up the flames of animosity.

The coach began his career with a newly completed baseball facility. Granted, the complex had serious flaws, but with work those problems would be overcome in years to come and by another coach. Dallas' leader was, to put things simply, lazy. He mowed the field with a bush hog. He dug out the warning track gravel and replaced it with mulch; the only apparent reason for doing so was that he would no longer have to kill the weeds. The trash drums were empty only when they would hold not one more cup or piece of paper. If he could convince his players or booster parents to do the job, he never touched the trash. As a result, animals such as dogs, skunks, and possums during the night often turned over the containers, and trash was blown across the entire facility.

Another problem was the man's temper. His fuse was short, and his personality was highly combustible. During games he frequently became irate, usually with one of his players, but sometimes with the progress of the game or an umpire's call. His neck turned scarlet as his anger increased, and he would erupt like a volcano. The coach often chewed boys out in such a loud manner that all in the stands could hear. During one of his last tantrums he threw a metal folding chair in the dugout, and it hit one of the players. The angered player picked the chair up and returned fire.

The worst quality of the coach was the fact that each year he selected one player whom the other players referred to as *the coach's whipping boy*. Whoever the boy might be, he could do nothing right; the coach constantly yelled at the player. He punished the athlete with limited playing time. At the beginning of each season, the coach told boys that they could always talk to him, but when one of the marked boys tried, the coach became angrier and refused to talk.

I attributed the problems that the coach had that final year of Dallas' career to the fact that his father died recently. His dad had been such a strong influence in his life that I supposed that the coach lost his sense of direction in life. His father's death had simply destroyed him. The anger that built inside the coach was poured onto that year's whipping boy. What made the year so bad was that Dallas became that whipping boy, and he suffered mightily as a result of it.

In the early season, Dallas was the starting first baseman. He played well in the field and made a few extraordinary plays in some games. He was making contact with the ball, but too often in the early part of the season he hit shots right to defensive players. As the year continued, his batting became stronger as he produced many excellent hits. In most games he would go one-for-three or two-for-five.

Too, Dallas pitched well in most games. He had a bad game against Heritage High School, but the team still managed to win. He didn't pitch well against Clinton High, but again the team won. The game that doomed him was one against West High School. On that day Dallas didn't have it. The other team hit him hard and often. Coach walked to the mound and began his tirade. Finally, he said,

You won't ever pitch again!

This he squalled loudly enough for both dugouts and the fans to hear. It was a way to belittle a player and to control him. Of course, the coach never remembered the games, such as the one against Oak Ridge, when Dallas had pitched well and won. He had forgotten when Dallas pitched against a private school with a team filled with college prospects and had shut them down, beaten them soundly. He stood by his word, however, and Dallas never pitched again.

Still, this group of boys for whom the coach had no special feelings finished the first half of the season undefeated in their district. The only comment from the coach was that he hoped they didn't fall apart the second half. Not one word of praise was given. Instead, he looked at this group as having been *lucky*.

The weekend of Easter was the beginning of the end of Dallas' season. The team traveled to Chattanooga for a weekend tournament. They played one night game at Soddy Daisy High School against a team from out-of-state. Our boys had played well, and we were beating the team. On one play a ground ball was hit to the shortstop, and he fielded the ball, but his throw was high and wide. Dallas couldn't catch the ball, but he hurried to retrieve the ball. He saw the runner advancing to third base. Dallas threw the ball, but the third baseman was unable to come up with the throw and allowed it to get by him. At the end of the inning the coach exploded on Dallas so badly that I was close to going after him. However, I knew that I would only embarrass Dallas by doing so. Now, not a word was said to the shortstop who made the wild throw. Nothing was mentioned to the third baseman about blocking up throws at his base. All the venom in the coach's being was spewed onto Dallas. From that night, Dallas never play first base again. Instead, the coach inserted a boy who had torn his rotator cuff. The guy couldn't throw the ball to third base at all; he had a difficult time taking infield. However, his dad was the scorekeeper, and he had done several favors for the coach. In the next game this boy made two costly errors at first base, but the coach only consoled him and patted him on the behind. Dallas, meanwhile, during his senior season, was the designated hitter. This boy, who the coach had the year before degraded for swinging hard, hit too well to be taken out of the line-up.

I went to the coach after a week or so, and I asked him why he wouldn't play Dallas anymore, but the coach refused to tell me, and he gave no answer when Dallas asked him. Instead, the other boy, a junior, played and continued to make errors each ballgame that hurt the team. Some of them cost the team wins.

I was furious, for my temper was one that was a match for the coach's. Parents and players alike asked me why Dallas wasn't playing, and I verbally abused the coach as I called him an incompetent idiot. He was putting the screw to my son for his own selfish reason. No one, I repeat, no one, could figure out what the coach was doing or why he was doing it. Dallas wore a bull's eye, and the coach was constantly sniping at him. He was the whipping boy of the 2003 season.

For one ball game Dallas's sister Lacey and her husband Nick were in attendance. Earlier in the day as I helped the coach to prepare the field for the game, I asked him if he would consider letting Dallas play that night. I had swallowed all my pride. I wanted Lacey to have one chance to see her brother play during his last year of baseball. That night when the line-up was announced, Dallas was still only the designated hitter; he would not play defense, and his sister never again saw him play.

From that point on, I stopped having any contact with the man. I did not speak to him unless I had to, and I berated him during each and every ballgame. I said things around him and waited for the end of the season so that I could confront this vindictive, heartless man.

Senior night came, and clouds gathered. Right before game time the rain came heavy for some time. When it ended, the coach decided to have the presentation of the seniors. The parents stood on the field, and as each player's name was called, the coach shook his hand, gave him a bat with his name on it and a flower to give to his mother. The entire affair was completed half-heartedly, and the players and parents were insulted. Again, this man's poor planning and laziness left no other choice for this game was the last home game, and it wasn't a game that counted in the standings for the end-of-season tournament. After the presentation, we parents prepared to watch the contest, but the coach called it because of the wet conditions. So, Dallas' senior night was a joke, anything but special.

By the end of the season the boys had lost their desire to play for this man, and they ended the season in a tie for the district championship. A coin toss gave top seeding to the other team, the one from which the coach had graduated, the one whose coach ours held up as god. In every one of those games, Dallas' replacement made at least one error. On two occasions those errors proved costly enough to lose games. Still, the coach petted him and ignored Dallas.

By this time Dallas had accepted his role. He said he would do everything he could to play, but he would not belittle himself by kissing the coach's ass. I told Dallas that after the season was over that I was going to have my say with the coach. Dallas looked at me and said,

It's all right, Dad. I don't care. Just leave it alone.

The team played the district tournament, and again we lost to the coach's alma mater. As a result, the boys played Farragut High School in the regional tournament. That year Farragut came in second in the state. The next two years it won the state championship. We packed our bags and went home.

Something that began thirteen years earlier suddenly was over. I wanted to cry, but I was so mad at the raw deal my son had received that I couldn't let the tears go. Maybe, though, what I was mad about was the fact that this incompetent coach had stolen the last year of baseball from me. I never again would watch Dallas play ball. He had no intentions of playing summer league and didn't want to tryout for any two- or four-year college teams. He just wanted it to be over.

I'd like to say life has been all smooth sailing since then, but that would be a lie. Dallas and I talk baseball, but for several years, the hurt was present and the wounds were still raw. I don't miss the anguish that accompanied the hundreds of games I watched and coached as Dallas played. I occasionally attend a game, but my interest is absent. I miss more than I can ever express watching my son, at any age, play a game at which he excelled. He suffered through the years with my chewing on him about something dealing with the game, but those things were also a part of life in general.

I wanted him to be a star in baseball. It didn't happen the way I had hoped. I wanted him to be a star in life. He is a success. I am humbled whenever I am introduced as Dallas Rector's dad. I am not so sure that Dallas has those same feelings about me. I know that he loves me. I hope that someday he understands what I tried to do during those years he played the game. I hope he someday has the opportunity to play ball with his son, and I hope that he learns from my mistakes what NOT to do.

I am proud of the man that Dallas has become. I look at him with awe. The hand of God touches him, and I am sure that the good Lord has special plans for him. I appreciate all that Dallas has done for me, and I hope that he can forgive me my shortcomings. They were all the products of a father's love.

AND NOW...

It's been several years since Dallas' last baseball game. Initially, I wasn't sure that I could survive without watching my son play the game that I love so well.

At the end of his senior season, I asked what he would do if a college coach showed some interest in him as a player. Dallas replied without hesitation,

I'd ask him how much money he was talking about.

Knowing that college coaches are notorious for giving partial scholarships to increase the number of players on the team, I asked Dallas,

You mean how much scholarship money the coach would be willing to give you?

His green eyes with brown flecks sparkled, and a grin crossed his face as he quipped,

No! I want to know how much money he's going to give me! Dad, it's over. I don't want to play ball in college. Classes will be hard enough without the pressure of playing baseball!

With that I knew without any doubt that baseball was over, at least in the way that I had known it for the last fourteen years. Dallas had completed his career, and as he always had done, he turned his attention in a different direction.

That first summer I imagined would be a terrible time as I suffered through the withdrawal of baseball from my life. Surprisingly, I discovered that much more time was available for other things. I didn't have to run around in a dither to complete the yard work before time to leave for a game. At night I could relax and enjoy a television show or read some of the books that I had discovered were so entertaining.

As life settled in the summer, I found that my personal life calmed as well. The fits of rage that I experienced during so many summer evenings were now over. No ballgame meant no aggravation. My life on the inside calmed. I felt much more at peace than ever before. No demons tortured me.

Dallas set out for new adventures for the summer. The first was a summer job. He worked at a plant that processed film. Each day he came home filthy from having handled the stuff. He complained incessantly about the working conditions, but I paid him little mind. I knew that his experiences there would only reinforce his resolve to earn a college degree. He also had time to spend with his friends. They actually found activities that fell outside the realm of baseball. In fact, I don't remember Dallas' picking up a bat, glove, or ball the entire summer.

Also to my surprise, I didn't really miss baseball. When the new school year began, I missed my son being at the same school everyday, but I didn't miss having to put up with the politics of the game. I was freed from having to be nice to a coach just so that Dallas wouldn't lose playing time. I could talk to him if I wanted, and I could ignore him as well.

Dallas and I experienced life after baseball. Times were awkward occasionally, but we worked through them. The subject that we avoided was baseball. His going away to college and beginning a new period in his life made things easier for him, and while I missed Dallas, my life without the game was much easier to handle.

In the spring of that first year Dallas asked how the team was doing, and I kept him updated on the scores and the wins and losses. I knew them because I read the sports section each day. During the entire season, I attended two games for a total of five innings. Without Dallas, I had little interest in the game or the team. The boy who had replaced Dallas the year before was now a senior and starting first baseman. I still held a grudge about past events, and I knew I was emotionally safer at home. That year the team performed horribly and had the first losing season for the coach during his tenure at the school.

By the end of the school year, the coach had been relieved of his duties and was reassigned to another school in the system. Too many things had piled up, and he couldn't get out from under them. Going to a new school and making a fresh start, as an assistant coach this time, was probably a good thing for the man. As I wrote this book, the steam that propelled my intense dislike of this coach lessened. Now, I don't care; baseball is far removed from my life, and my son and family survived the rocky roads that high school ball presented. I don't feel the hate; I am indifferent now.

A couple of summers after high school, Dallas and I completed what he called a "pilgrimage" to Durham, North Carolina. There we spent three days touring the campus of Duke University. We both are avid fans of the Blue Demons in general and Coach K in particular. Luckily, Dallas was able to walk onto the floor at Cameron Arena. He immediately struck up a conversation with a man, and Dallas told him we had traveled the distance just to see the facility. The man threw him a basketball and told Dallas to shoot as long as he wanted to. I stood under the goal for one and a half hours and rebounded for him as he shot. At one point, Dallas looked at me and said,

"This is the greatest thing that has ever happened in my life!"

The trip to Duke helped us to reconnect, and since then we have been more like a father and son should be.

Dallas and I have begun to talk about baseball again. He met the new coach, and I have kept him informed on the team's progress. All of the sources of pain are gone. I've attended three games this year, and during one of them I stood with the boy who had replaced Dallas during his senior year. We talked amiably, and I enjoyed the time. I didn't dislike him any more. Baseball was over; it returned to just a game. Dallas and I have made tentative plans to watch the minor league teams in Knoxville and Chattanooga during the summer. We might even journey to Atlanta for a game or two and cover a lot of miles to watch the college world series. To be truthful, our main objective is to drive to Moreland, Georgia, the birthplace of one of our favorite celebrities, Lewis Grizzard.

Dallas also stepped out a little by joining a fraternity. I have never liked those organizations, but that is a long story about a different time in life. As strange as it sounds, I am tremendously proud that he joined the organization. He did something for himself. He showed me that he could love me without having to always agree with everything I think or say. Before long, he got out of the fraternity scene because of the crazy drinking and antics of members. That included him at one point, but he grew tired of it. Sure enough, he was quickly becoming a man.

Times weren't all roses for Dallas. Between baseball and his dad, he fought every day to believe in himself. He was so afraid of failure or of letting his parents down that he often told us what he thought we wanted to hear instead of what the truth was. As a result, he's made some mistakes in his college classes, and he fell behind for a while. With the help of some good people who listened objectively to him, Dallas shook the fog from his mind and began to have a more positive outlook about himself. He then headed in the right direction and looks forward to life since he graduated from college and began looking for a career. Go get 'em, Tiger!!

Maybe I am finally growing up too. Granted, the hour in my life is late, but I can be at peace for the rest of my time. I've learned so much over the years, but I've learned it all so slowly. I know that baseball is a game, one for kids and not their parents. I understand that all of my *want to* never can cause another person to perform a single act. I realize how fortunate I am that Dallas is understanding and forgiving. He has given me chance after chance; he has stuck with me, even when I haven't deserved his loyalty.

I coached the high school fall ball team when the most recent coach came to Karns, and while I had fun, I saw the end of my coaching days. I don't have the energy for the job, and something is missing when Dallas isn't there. I officially resigned from coaching duties. From now on, I am going to be a spectator who watches the game and marvels at the players' abilities. The next time I scream at Dallas, I will do so in order for him to find me in a crowded stadium.

The most rewarding thing that Dallas has said occurred recently. On one of our days of hanging out together, the subject of baseball came up. The school team had enjoyed a winning streak, and I related their good fortunes to Dallas. He listened to me, and after a lapse in the conversation, Dallas said, "I didn't think I'd ever say it, but I miss playing baseball."

That was enough for me. It was all right for us to go back to the game we spent so much time with a long while ago. We watch games on television and read clippings in the paper. Baseball has once again become a game, something that a father and son can enjoy without having any pressure. It took long enough, but I finally got it! Thank goodness!

THE FEELINGS
CONTINUE

Not long ago, I took a trip to Powell Levi Fields. It's a collection of baseball/ softball fields not far from the house. Dallas had played on those fields when he moved to competitive league teams. The community is proud of the complex, and parent sweat equity has maintained them. On most days through the week and even on weekends, the parking lot is filled, as are the fields. Children as young as four and as old as twelve play league and tournament games right on through the month of October.

The reason for my driving to the field was to watch one of those games. My nephew Brandon has a son Caden, who turned four recently. He's on one of the t-ball teams in that league. I was excited to hear that the boy was playing and looked forward to an opportunity to see him in action. I felt sure it would be a wonderful time that would be filed with fun. WRONG!

Also in attendance at the game were my brother Jim and his wife Brenda, proud and doting grandparents, Caden's mother and sister, and his other grandfather. Brandon had taken a day off from his second shift job so that he could take Caden to the game. By the time I arrived, Brandon and his son were in the outfield, and dad was hitting grounders to son. His abilities stood out for all to see. Already at the age of four the boy could stop a ground ball and make a strong, accurate throw to his dad. It had to be some kind of innate ability because the child looked eerily like his dad on the field. He is a small child, short in stature with well-defined muscles, every bit the same as his dad was during those years. As he ran, I flashed back to scene of Brandon at that age, and a smile crossed my lips.

The entire time the two of them were playing, not a cross word was spoken. Brandon calmly instructed as to what he should do, and the boy gave every effort to oblige. Plenty of praise followed good plays, and positive instruction came after mistakes.

As soon as the game began, my nerves set on edge. Caden was playing second base and stopped every ball thrown to him in warm up. Then the first batter for the other team stepped to the plate. He swung at a pitch, and the weight of the bat spun him around and almost dropped him to the ground. I smiled and thought "how cute these little players are." The second pitch headed toward the plate and the batter again swung with all his might; the result was a swinging bunt. The pitcher, shortstop, and Caden converged on the ball, and by the time the pitcher wrestled it from other two, the batter stood on second and flashed a smiled at his mom in the stands.

Those old feelings rumpled in my gut and began the ascent to my head. Before long, I yelled out to Caden: "keep your butt down," watch it all the way in," and "pay attention." My squalling surprised me when I became aware of it. Old habits die hard, and I realized that every muscle in my body was tensed as if a punch were coming toward my solar plexus.

Once again in control of my emotions, as well as my big mouth, I watched the game. On several occasions, the urge to yell instructions to Caden came, but they were squelched. It helped that I viewed the entire game from the confines of the center field fence. Caden hit the ball well and made some good plays, but I couldn't enjoy the game. Once at home, I plopped down exhausted in my recliner and sat there the rest of the evening. No player expended more energy than I had as I fretted and fussed and fumed over a t-ball game. It was obvious that I hadn't conquered the demons that wreaked so much havoc a few years earlier. The only way to keep it away was by avoiding ball games altogether, at least the ones where a family member was a player.

Grandson Madden played his first organized game at the age of three—SOCCER. His parents were excited, and I was too. They allowed me to purchase his uniform that year. Amy and I traveled to Nashville to watch him play. The weather was raw, and the wind blew like a hurricane. I stood on the sidelines with camera ready to snap shots of every minute of exciting play. Over a hundred photos were taken, but few of them included Madden's star performance.

In the ones I viewed, my grandson cared little about the game. Sometimes he decided he'd rather check out what was going on with folks on the sidelines. Other times, Madden stood in the middle of the field and watched the action. He made no attempt to kick the ball or defend his goal. For one period, blades of grass held his attention more than the game.

The fact that Madden was three mitigated nothing for me. I encouraged him to participate, but when he turned a blind eye and a deaf ear to me, my blood boiled. The old feelings rose in me. My grandson should be a leader on the team. He needed to run and kick and score and defend. That's the way the game is played, and I expected him to get with the program. Goofing off was for other kids.

Then it hit me like a meteor falling from the sky. Madden hadn't even turned three. Here is a two-year-old playing on an organized soccer team. Hell, he still wore a diaper at night. His attention span equaled that of a puppy. He learned to kick the ball, to run on the field, and to have fun with new friends. Most of all, he enjoyed just being there. All the other stuff about soccer and baseball comes in time, unless overly demanding parents and coaches make a sport a chore instead of a fun activity.

The last game of the year, Madden scored two goals, the only ones from the season. The marvelous thing about those scores is that the coach worked with older boys on the team so that they could help him score. They dribbled the ball toward the goal and to the spot where Madden was positioned. Then they passed the ball to him and told him to kick it in the goal. It was the grandest display of team play and sportsmanship I've ever heard about. And it all occurred with kids working together with a good coach who identifies his job as developing skills of all players. I'm thankful that Madden played for such a wonderful leader and more thankful that I don't live close enough to watch every game and either become too involved or vocal. Let him play and let me keep my mouth shut. That's the way everyone will find happiness.

ABOUT THE AUTHOR

Joe Rector retired after 30 years as a high school English teacher. He's written columns for three different newspapers. No Right Field for My Son is his second book. Baseball Boys is available through Amazon.com and at e-book sites. He also maintains his blog, www.thecommonisspectacular.com, where he posts weekly columns covering a variety of topics. Contact him for more information and to send your comments at joerector@comcast.net.